How Do You Do, My Name is Sue!

a memoir

Susanah K. Pratt

How Do You Do, My Name is Sue!

Copyright © 2023 by Susanah K. Pratt

All rights reserved.

Published by Red Penguin Books

Bellerose Village, New York

ISBN

Print 978-1-63777-486-1

Digital 978-1-63777-469-4

No part of this book may be reproduced in any form or by any electronic or mechanical means, including information storage and retrieval systems, without written permission from the author, except for the use of brief quotations in a book review.

Dedicated to my husband
George C Pratt

Without your love and interest this book wouldn't
have been completed.
Thank you!
Love u forever!

Sue

CONTENTS

	Prologue	1
1.	Last Christmas	3
2.	Waiting for Word	9
3.	Who is Sue?	15
4.	Twenty Years as Housewife and Mother	29
5.	A New Year & New Experiences	47
6.	Jim	55
7.	Juggling Kids, a Job & College	59
8.	A Feeling of Accomplishment	67
9.	Bermuda	73
10.	Frequent Flier	83
11.	My Ever-Expanding Family	87
12.	A Unique Yacht Cruise	97
13.	Happy Birthday to Me	103
14.	Many Blessings	107
15.	China for One	113
16.	Africa	119
17.	South America	125
18.	A Truly Special Traveling Companion	131
19.	Places I Would Like to See	137
20.	Iceland	145
21.	Second Marriage at 85	149
22.	Our One-year Wedding Anniversary!	155
23.	Alaska	159
24.	Reflections	163
25.	And In Conclusion	171
	Epilogue	173

PROLOGUE

Before I graduated high school, I was already wearing an engagement ring. My two older brothers had attended Dad's alma mater, Michigan State University. Dad felt a girl didn't need a college education to get a "Mrs." in front of her name. All she had to do was find a good husband, and she would be set for life.

My husband, Charlie, a graduate of Officer Candidate School (OCS) and a new Second Lieutenant for the U.S. Army in Field Artillery, returned from Korea in 1953, unhurt and better off for the experience. Press the fast forward button twenty years ahead. There were four babies in five years, a mortgage on a small two-bedroom Cape Cod in Long Island, and a tight budget. I loved being a mom, and life was good.

We were all shocked when Charlie had a heart attack at age thirty-nine. I didn't know it then, but a major change was coming for our family. And it had nothing to do with Charlie's coronary issues.

CHAPTER 1
LAST CHRISTMAS

Christmas was very special to my husband, Charlie, and to me. On the coldest, windiest day in December of 1972 at One Underhill Avenue in Syosset New York, Charlie climbed up the big ladder, carrying strings of colored lights. He started at the rooftop peak and attached the green electric cords to the roof. They flowed along the ridge of the house and down to the breezeway and onto the garage roof. A perfect outline of our cozy Cape Cod house, "little house, you are really very small, just big enough for love, that's all." A large, live evergreen wreath, complete with a big red bow, hung on our front door.

Inside, the house was filled with the wonderful aromas of a stuffed roasted turkey and homemade apple pie as we prepared for a large Christmas gathering of family and friends. In the kitchen, we were finishing up the shrimp cocktails. Three large, cooked shrimp clung to the edge of each goblet. Shredded lettuce and cocktail sauce, (ketchup and horseradish), waited to be topped with a lemon slice and cold shrimp. Fresh apple cider from the local Jericho Cider Mill, mashed potatoes with gravy, yummy stuffing, favorite vegetables like Aunt Norm's carrots, green bean casserole, broccoli souffle, corn, and dinner rolls graced the table.

The fold-up tables, borrowed from the Community Church, were placed end to end and extended from the wall in the small dining area into the living room. We'd also borrowed from the church a bunch of fold-up chairs. It would be crowded but cozy. The lace tablecloth, complete with red-and-green, holly-patterned napkins was the perfect background for glowing balsam-scented candles. Christmas music came from our brand new HiFi phonograph.. (Remember how they could play several 78 rpm records at one time?)

Charlie had ongoing projects both inside and outside the house. Upstairs, he had already completed two bedrooms, a bathroom, and a cedar closet. He was also working on the new kitchen cabinet doors. The basement "family" room, with wood paneling and tile floor, was almost finished.

This was my thirty-ninth Christmas and my twenty-second with Charlie, whom I had met at a church dance when I was in the eighth grade. Three of our four children were now teenagers; Cheryl, our eldest, was seventeen and a senior in high school, Linda, a sophomore, was fifteen. Thirteen-year-old Lori had just started the ninth grade, and Charles, our youngest, was twelve and was entering junior high school.

This year, there were twelve place settings at our holiday table. In addition to our family of six, Charlie's mother, Minnie, was there, along with my parents, Grandma and Grandpa Earl and Susannah Mallison, who had driven up from their home in Washington, D.C. to spend the week of Christmas and New Year's with us. That made nine. Linda had invited her boyfriend Eddie to join us, too. We also had Tom Hunter, the youth pastor at our church, and Mrs. Eckert.

Cheryl was a "candy striper" volunteer aide in the local nursing home and didn't want one of the patients there, Mrs. Eckert, to be alone at Christmas time. Linda was the one who'd invited Mr. Hunter. She'd discovered that he was not going home to

Massachusetts for Christmas, so he joined us, too. There was always room for one more at the table.

Conversation stopped as everybody was enjoying the food. The only sounds you heard were "Please pass the potatoes," and "Is there anymore in the kitchen?"

We moved into the living room for dessert and coffee and the opening of our Christmas presents. Laughter and love filled the air.

Mrs. Eckert seemed especially pleased. "This is real coffee, isn't it?" she remarked, holding the cup under her nose to savor the aroma of the freshly brewed beans.

I guess they only served instant coffee at the nursing home.

Our bellies full, Charlie led us down the basement stairs to our new, dark-paneled walls and tiled floor of the family room, complete with a set of "modern" furniture. Money was tight, but Charlie had a vision for our little home, and he was slowly making it happen. He'd done all the work himself, with his brother, Harry lending a hand on the weekends.

Harry was a draftsman for an architect, and he was a perfectionist, just like everyone else in Charlie's family, so the two men focused on doing everything correctly, which, to my chagrin, added to the length of every project. Still, it was a wonderful trait. Charlie wanted the best for his family, and he was eager to create for us the home he believed we deserved.

Charlie was excited to show off his latest project, but also, he couldn't stop talking about his upcoming trip to Miami for the Orange Bowl college football game. He had never been to one of the big games and was happily talking about the teams that would be competing four days later. Tom played his guitar while we sang Christmas and other songs.

With a flurry of "Happy New Year" wishes to everyone, all but my parents left. They said good night to us and climbed two sets of stairs to our guest bedroom. I remember thinking it was well worth all the effort to have such a special family time. The words of the original song that Tom sang came into my mind, *"So close your eyes and lean back here against me, you've seen the good times, you've seen the rain come down..."*

Last known picture of Charlie - 1971

We didn't know this would be our last Christmas with Charlie.

The next few days found us cleaning the house, putting away the "good" dishes, returning the folding tables and chairs to the church, enjoying turkey sandwiches, and thinking about the New Year, 1973.

After dinner on Friday, December 29th, Charlie hugged us and said goodbye. I watched from the front door as he put his small carry-on bag in the back seat of his 1965, dark green Mustang. He waved and backed out of the driveway for what would be the last time.

I felt a sudden shiver, as a very dark feeling entered my mind.

Early in the morning of December 30, I was in the basement starting a load of laundry.

THE TELEPHONE RANG. I quickly picked up the extension. The rest of the family was still sleeping. It was my daughter's boyfriend, Eddie. He'd remembered Charlie's excitement about the upcoming Orange Bowl and knew he was flying out a few days after our holiday dinner.

"Mrs. Kuchenbrod, which flight did your husband take to Miami?" he asked.

I wasn't sure, I told him, but I thought it was Eastern Flight 401 out of John F. Kennedy Airport.

There was no response. Dead silence.

I asked, "Eddie, why do you want to know?"

Eddie's father worked for British Airways. His dad had heard one of the first bulletins announcing that a large jet plane had crashed in the Everglades and rescue efforts were underway.

I think now, in retrospect, at that moment I knew Charlie wasn't coming home.

Slowly climbing the stairs, I entered the living room and turned on the television. My dad had just finished his morning exercise and joined me as we waited for more news. But the early reports were very sketchy, and the news media didn't really know anything yet.

I finally called Eastern Airlines hoping for more details. The airline representative couldn't tell me much. But she recommended I take the next available flight to Miami and told me not to worry about a ticket. She said something about arranging for a "non-revenue" voucher.

I called my in-laws to tell them about the frightening news. They were traumatized. My mother-in-law, Minnie, was having trouble accepting the fact that "Charles" might not be coming home. She needed her other son, Harry, and younger daughter, Florence, to be with her.

But who was going to Miami? Not knowing what the outcome would be, I knew I was the one to go. I thought my children and my parents needed to be together. Both of my brothers lived out of state. Going alone seemed to be the best solution.

We were all in shock. But I worked hard to keep my composure. I didn't want to alarm the kids. We had no idea if Charlie had survived the crash, but I was holding out hope for the children and for me.

I told the kids that Eastern Airlines had recommended I come down to Miami. If their dad was in the hospital, there would be a real person there to take care of him.

My thoughts while packing my suitcase centered on Charlie. I remembered the presents he'd bought for me, a beautiful silk-like Loden green raincoat with matching hat, plaid slacks from Bloomingdales, a cashmere sweater, feminine blouses and nightwear. I also remembered that in November, near our 20th wedding anniversary, he had called to ask me for a date for dinner.

I was all in a dither, wondering what to wear, what we would say. That night, he gave me a gold bracelet that I will always treasure. Late that afternoon, I arrived at Kennedy Airport, where I boarded the plane with only a small carry-on bag. I was escorted to a window seat. The flight attendants knew why I was alone, and they made every effort to comfort me. Although I was thirty-nine, I had flown only once before in my life, to Ann Arbor, Michigan, so that I could attend my cousin Jeanne's wedding.

I stared out the window as we took off and began our flight south toward Miami. It was getting dark out, and I thought about how small everything appeared. At night, the shining lights below sparkled like beautiful gems scattered on a piece of black velvet cloth.

I rested my head against the window and overheard the woman seated behind me tell her small son to stop pushing his feet on the back of my seat. He stopped. Then I heard him turn in his seat as he leaned over to look out the window.

In a small, sweet voice, he softly sang to himself, "Jesus loves me, this I know, for the Bible tells me so." I knew then I could cope with whatever the future would bring.

CHAPTER 2
WAITING FOR WORD

Even back then, 1972, Miami International was a very large and busy airport. I found my way to the passenger pick-up area and waited for Jim Jester.

Jim was a former co-worker of Charlie's who had recently transferred to Miami. Jim would drive me to the hospital, where I hoped to find out whether my husband had survived and was being brought in for treatment of his injuries.

It was not warm, as I'd always imagined Florida to be, but a cool, rainy afternoon. Leaving the airport, I noticed communities of small homes decorated for the holidays. As we entered the highway, I saw Christmas lights hung in the palm trees. A light rain slowed our progress but soon we arrived at Miami Memorial Hospital. It was not only a hospital, but a morgue and a repository for official records.

Miami Memorial became the command center for the accident. By the time I arrived, the television news programs were filled with reports about the crash—but with few details about what had happened because the incident had occurred deep in the Everglades, and it was difficult for emergency workers to reach the site.

The plane was one of Eastern's newest, a Lockheed L-1011 TriStar that carried 163 passengers. It had only been delivered to the airline four months earlier in August 1972.

Many wondered why it had crashed as it was a clear, moonless night. According to news reports, as the plane had approached the Miami airport, the pilot noticed that one of the cockpit lights failed to turn on and signal that the nose landing gear had locked into place. He obtained permission from the control tower to circle out over the Everglades, west of Miami, while they tried to fix the problem.

The Everglades are uninhabited, so there were no lights on the ground and the night was dark and moonless. In the confusion, apparently one of the crew accidentally hit the auto-pilot descend button. The pilot and crew were busy concentrating on the landing-gear problem and did not notice that the plane was gradually descending. In the darkness there were no visual clues to identify the ground. In the end, the plane simply flew into the Everglades' swamp at 250 MPH.

We later learned that three of the four cockpit crew members, two of the ten flight attendants, and 96 of the 163 passengers had died. Also killed were the pilot, Captain Robert Albin (Bob) Loft, and second officer Donald Repro There were 75 survivors.

The final decision about the cause of the accident was recorded as "pilot error."

Author John Fueller would write a nonfiction book based on the disaster and, in particular, about Second Officer Repro, entitled *The Ghost of Flight 401,* that was released in 1978. Later that year, the book would be made into a feature film starring Ernest Borgnine, Gary Lockwood, Tina Chen and Kim Bassinger.

Once at the hospital, Red Cross workers took us to an area where other friends and relatives of the passengers were waiting. As information was minimal, the workers suggested we accept rooms in nearby local motels, provided by Eastern Airlines. Certainly, we could watch local television and hear more up-to-date information. So, Jim Jester escorted me there.

I thought of my family. I called home and spoke with my children. My mom told me they were doing okay. She also told me she had called my brother, Bob, who lived in Orlando, and he was on his way to meet me.

I stayed up through the night but still didn't learn anything about my husband, Charlie Kuchenbrod. Jim stayed at the hotel with me, but when I learned my brother Bob was coming, I insisted he go home. I really needed to use the toilet, so he left.

Jim later told me his wife "gave him hell for leaving me." It was the wee hours in the morning that Bob knocked on the door. I was very happy to see him.

The next morning Bob, Jim and I returned to the same waiting room at the hospital. It wasn't as crowded as the night before. But information was still slow in coming in, and the morning dragged on. I needed to take a walk, get some fresh air, maybe get some lunch.

We prayed for good news and returned to the waiting area.

It felt like hours had passed when I heard the name "KUCHENBROD" called. I looked up and saw a man from the hospital holding something in his hand. The man then gave me a very wet wallet, Charlie's wedding ring, and the car keys for his Mustang. He asked if my husband had any identifying scars, or unusual birthmarks. Funny, I could not think of any. He said a visual identification was required. I was in shock and wondered if I could do it. Bob turned to me and said, "Sue, I will do it," and left with the man.

It wasn't too long before Bob returned and told me there was no doubt; it was Charlie who'd been found dead. He said there was a head wound, indicating he had sustained a major blow to his brow. The final cause of death was listed as "multiple body injuries, severe."

After all the survivors of the plane crash had been found and whisked away for treatment, the search for the victims was begun. It was then that Charlie's body was found amid the wreckage.

Bodies were identified, tagged, put into catastrophe bags, and stored in refrigerated trucks. I like to think that because Charlie was one of the last passengers to be identified, he was among the first to be picked up. That helped me later when Cheryl, who went on to attend nursing school in Hartford, Connecticut, said she had read that some of the passengers had been eaten by alligators.

It was New Year's Eve and I wanted to go home to be with my family. Severe fog had socked in most northeastern airports. The staff from Eastern Airlines said they would get me to New York, even if I were the only passenger on the plane.

Better heads prevailed. Bob suggested we go to Orlando and fly home to New York in the morning. My sister-in-law, Esther, offered medication but I wanted a clear head.

We were on the first flight to Kennedy Airport. It was a beautiful warm, sunny day. We found Charlie's dark green Mustang in the JFK parking lot. Even though there was a representative from Eastern Airlines there to explain why we didn't have the parking lot receipt, the attendant refused to let the vehicle go. No ticket, no car.

Bob said that when he flew, he generally put his parking stub in his wallet, so he suggested maybe Charlie did the same. We peeled through each layer of the wet items and found the ticket.

Back at home, our family, friends, and many from the community reached out and provided more comfort than they will ever know.

Our pastor, Malcom "Mal" Bertram, stayed with our family. Pastor Mal, as he was affectionately known, had come to our church, the Community Church of Syosset, just two years earlier in 1970. His former church was in Garden City—not Garden City, Long Island, but Garden City, Kansas.

Despite the geographic adjustment, Pastor Mal, his wife Barbara and their family easily settled into life in suburbia. Syosset's population was increasing, as was the Community Church membership, and Mal eagerly accepted the challenge. During his tenure, Mal transformed the church's type of governing body from a representative two boards (like our National Government) to a town meeting style with a Board of Stewards. He also expanded the choir—a new piano was a noticeable asset—and hired an inspiring Director of Music.

There were four full-time staff members, Mal, Fred Bachman, Tom Hunter, and Jean Butler. (In 1972-73 I served an intentional one year term as Administrator of Christian Education.)

Pastor Mal was full of confidence and attended all the Board of Elders meetings dressed in a plaid jacket, blue slacks, a 'clergy' shirt, and Peace emblem on a gold chain around his neck. Many associated the peace emblem with the 'hippies.'

It was the early '70s, a time Social Commentator Tom Wolfe called the "me decade." The Vietnam War was raging, and America's youth was out in the streets protesting our country's involvement. Richard Nixon was the president and bell bottoms pants, midi and mini dresses, headbands and tie-dyed clothing were all the rage. And Mal embraced the times and the younger members of our congregation.

He told me later he had never before prayed with and thoughtfully tucked three adolescent girls into bed. The night after Charlie's death had been a first for him. His suggestion that we leave the Christmas lights on as a tribute to Charlie was truly inspirational. Later, people told me it was a real message of hope.

A memorial service was held at our family church, the Community Church of Syosset. The candles on the altar and the Christmas decorations of red poinsettia plants and dark green wreaths hung on each window were a comforting sight.

There was a big turnout, and the crowd overflowed the sanctuary. Chairs were added, and others stood. The large choir provided their music to the service. The current style was long dresses and Cheryl, Linda and Lori wore their Christmas outfits.

As we were about to leave the service, I noticed Hank Sinnegan, a former boss of Charlie's, and a good friend. He was facing the front of the church toward the white, cloth-covered casket. Slowly his hand rose, and he saluted as he said, "So long, Charlie."

It was then I realized that Charlie was really gone.

My parents stayed in New York for my daughters' birthdays, Cheryl's on January 6, and Linda's five days later, on the eleventh. Then, they returned home to Washington, D.C.

My dad got into the driver's seat, and my mom slowly made her way around to the passenger side of the car. She looked back at me, paused, then waved. Some months later, she confided that leaving me standing there alone on the driveway next to my four children was the most difficult thing she had ever experienced. But for me, being on my own was the best decision. I needed to test my strength. And I knew my parents were just a short flight away if I needed them.

That January, the children reluctantly returned to school. A different life had begun for my family and me.

CHAPTER 3
WHO IS SUE?

I was midway through the eighth grade when I first met Charlie. It was 1946, World War II had just ended, and my father accepted a job in New York City. Until then, we had always been following my dad's military postings and moving from place to place.

At nineteen, I had gone from my parents' home to my married home. Now, for the very first time, I would be on my own. At thirty-nine, I was widowed with four children, a house and a mortgage. Without Charlie, it was all up to me. I could either sink or swim.

Of course, I would swim. I was my mother's daughter, after all. Although she was married, she was often raising us kids on her own. Dad was a good husband and father, but there were many times as a military man, he was called away and she was forced to raise us kids on her own. Looking back, I am certain that her strength had helped me to be strong.

Born in Chicago Heights, Illinois, in 1903, my mother, Susannah (nee Herschberger) Hoover, was the third of four daughters born to Libby Darling (nee Page) and William Harrison Hoover. (Yes, according to family lore, America's 31st President, Herbert Hoover, is a very distant relative.)

I don't know much about my mom's early life, or if she even graduated from high school. I do know that she worked for a time as a switchboard operator at the Battle Creek Sanitarium, a world-renowned health resort in Battle Creek. She was the only one of the four sisters to leave Michigan. She met my father, Earl Dewey Mallison, a military man five years her senior, on a blind date.

Born in 1889 on a farm in Hesperia, Michigan, my father was the eldest of Emma and Frank Mallison's three sons. After attending a one-room schoolhouse, his benevolent grandmother let him live with her in neighboring Shelby, where he attended high school. She then lent him money to attend Michigan Agriculture College in East Lansing, which is now Michigan State University.

Dad joined the Army's ROTC, or Reserve Officers Training Corps. After graduating during the last year of World War 1, he was sent, as a 2nd Lieutenant in the Army Reserve, to Camp Custer in Battle Creek, the birthplace of the cereal industry, where he met my mother.

Near the end of World War I, the United States Department of Agriculture offered Dad a job in Washington, D.C, which he accepted. In 1925, my parents were married in my grandparents' home, and he and Mom settled in the D.C. area.

Sue's parents, Susannah Herschberger Hoober Mallison and Earl Dewey Malison in 1979

Dad's job after WW I with the Department of Agriculture was in the area of research and development. He also continued his duties with the ROTC. Mom gave birth to two sons, Robert, a.k.a. "Bob," in Washington, D.C., and to Joe in Yakima in the state of Washington.

In 1930, Dad's work took the family to Yakima. The state of Washington is known for its excellent apples and potatoes. Part of his research was to try to determine the best way to ship produce, while retaining the quality of the item. He sailed by freighter from California to the east coast to record the actual effects of changes in temperature and the various shipping containers on the produce. He was then reassigned to Washington, D.C.

When Mom found a friend, Mrs. Tisdale, who wanted to visit Battle Creek, she decided to drive home for a visit. Then she would meet Dad in Washington D.C. She took the two boys, ages six and three, and accompanied by Mrs. Tisdale, she drove from California to her hometown in their new car, a two-door, 1931 Ford coupe, complete with a running board. (A running board is a step located below the car door that enables one to easily step into or out of the car.)

Soon after she arrived in Michigan, she discovered that she was pregnant again—a fine mess to be in with her husband away working and she alone with two very young boys. Following the old wives' tale that if she boiled onions in vinegar and stood over the vapors, it would abort the baby, she began to heat up some vinegar. But her oldest sister persuasively begged her, "Susan, stop, it might be a little girl."

It was a typical hot August day. My mother lay on a rubber sheet on a bed in Garfield Hospital. Her obstetrician was listening on the radio to the baseball game. The Washington Senators were winning! The baby girl could wait no longer, and on August 5, 1933, I joined the Mallison family.

I arrived during a bleak time in history. Franklin Delano Roosevelt had recently defeated Herbert Hoover as President. Nineteen-thirty-three was one of the worst years of the Great Depression. The whole world was suffering from high unemployment. Adolph Hitler had just been appointed chancellor of Germany; he banned all other political parties, turning Germany into a one-party state. He also opened the first concentration camp, Dachau. And, here in the U.S., strong winds, poor farming techniques, and a severe drought forced many people to leave the "dust bowl" and seek work and find homes in other parts of the country.

Certificate of Birth Registration

This is to Certify, That in accordance with an Act to provide for the better registration of births in the District of Columbia and for other purposes, approved March 1, 1907, the birth of a Female child to Earl D. and Susanah H. Mallison on August 5, 1933 has been officially registered in the Health Office of the District of Columbia, by Dr. W. Sinclair Bowen

Record No. 361,412 Name of Child Susanah Ellen

M. D.,
Health Officer.

To Mrs. Earl Mallison
103 Virginia Avenue
Jefferson Park, Alexandria, Va.

FORM #79 GARFIELD MEMORIAL HOSPITAL — OBSTETRICAL DEPARTMENT
Name of Mother Mrs. Susanah Mallison
Date of Birth 8-5-33 Hour of Birth 6:27 p.m.
Sex of Infant Female
Left FOOTPRINT OF INFANT Right

Sue's birth certificate – August 5, 1933

My parents were happy to have a daughter; I am not too sure about my two big brothers. And, to this day, onions and vinegar are not a problem for me! As the youngest, and the only girl, I was a little bit of a spoiled brat. With two older brothers, I grew up as "Sissy."

By the late 1930s, there were rumblings of war emanating from Europe. In 1939, Dad was ordered to Fort Benning, Georgia, for upgraded training methods, and the family joined him there. After his three months training, we moved near Hyattsville, Maryland, the new home of the Research Department of the Department of Agriculture.

I was young, but I vividly remember December 7, 1941. It was Sunday, and Dad, my two brothers and I set out just after lunch to cut down an evergreen tree for Christmas. We hiked to a wooded area just across the road from our house and began our search. Happily, we found a tree that was nicely sized and shaped. We cut it down and dragged it across the field toward home. Nearing the house, we could see Mom on the front lawn frantically calling out to us.

"Pearl Harbor has been bombed!" she shouted.

The Japanese Naval Service had bombed our naval base in Honolulu, Hawaii. The entire nation was shocked. War with Japan was imminent. As a member of the ROTC, Dad was immediately called to active duty and ordered to Camp Wheeler, the Infantry Replacement Center in Georgia, where he was to learn upgraded training methods. He was destined to train future soldiers.

Here at home, air raid practice, blackout shades, rationing of many items became the norm. Victory gardens, recycling tin cans, and using fake butter helped us feel we were doing our part in the war effort. Every school-age child wore a metal ID tag on a chain. At school, when the alarm sounded, we dove under our desks.

Recognizing that Dad's work and army duties through the ROTC would require him to move again and again, my parents decided to keep the family together as much as possible. During America's engagement in World War II, we moved from rented house to rented house five times. Each time Dad was transferred, Mom would wait for the school year to end before we would pack up to join him.

The impacts of those frequent moves on the family weren't lost on anyone. But Mom was courageous and strong, always caring for my brothers and me. We stayed in Maryland until the school year was over before moving to Macon, Georgia, to be near Dad.

The three-bedroom house he rented for us had a full, covered front porch with white pillars. It was settled in the middle of a large, green lawn surrounded with a white picket fence. I loved the front double swinging gates. Each room had its own fireplace for heat. There was no basement, and the foundation was on cinder blocks. We lived there for two years.

Dad was transferred to Camp Blanding, Florida. Mom and us

kids were set to join him at the end of the school year, but the house he had rented for us in Gainesville would not be ready until the Fall. So, we got to spend the summer of 1943 at a beach colony on Anastasia Island, near Saint Augustine, where Dad rented a bungalow.

I'm not sure how he found this place (he was busy training soldiers) but my beach companion that summer was a boy named Phil, who happened to be the general's son. Anastasia Island was pretty barren. There were no lifeguards at the beach, so during the day, my brothers were supposed to watch over me. But I didn't like their favorite activity—fishing. While my brothers fished off a nearby pier, I rode the waves on air-filled Army mattress covers.

The pier was also a favorite haunt for the local shark fishermen who baited a large hook with a piece of beef. One day they caught a shark, pulled it up on the pier and then slit the belly open. Out popped numerous small fish and debris. The shark liver oil and sharkskin brought the fishermen a good price.

When we visited a nearby alligator zoological farm, we came upon a black-skinned employee sitting on the back of an alligator. I asked if he was afraid that he'd be eaten.

He replied, "No ma'am, they don't like dark meat."

The country's oldest masonry fort, Castillo de San Marcos, built of coquina stone, is located in Saint Augustine, near the Ponce de Leon Bridge. Coquina is composed of fossilized fragments of shells that were so hard they caused cannon shells to bounce off. The fort was never captured. If the British, during the French and Indian War, had captured Florida earlier, much earlier than 1763, it might have changed the course of the American Revolution. Maybe our country, like Canada, would still be part of the British Empire.

One summer, I learned that my best friend Ann was going to Girl Scout camp. I was excited when I found out that I could join her.

Eight of us slept on cots in a wooden cabin with screened windows. After taps, we went to bed and the chatter began.

Because it was wartime, stories began circulating about our cabin being surrounded by Japanese soldiers, and everyone agreed they were after me, because my dad was an Army officer. I was frightened and asked Ann if I could sleep with her. The next day, one of the counselors drove me home, hoping I would feel better after seeing my mom. When I learned that the plan was for me to return to camp that afternoon, I balked. No way! So, I stayed at the beach with my mom and brothers.

In September, we moved from the beach colony into the house in Gainesville. My brothers were in high school. I was still in elementary school and was soon busy with activities and new friends. I attended P.K. Yonge Laboratory School, which was connected to the University of Florida. They introduced me at an early age to typing, foreign language, and other innovative programs.

While we were living in Gainesville, some Sunday mornings would find Dad and me riding bikes around the University of Florida's campus. There were orange groves along many of the roads we'd ride on, and we would often come upon small orange juice stands with signs that read, "All you can drink—five cents." Bike riding became a wonderful sport for me.

Dinnertime, especially on Sundays, was family time. Another cup of tea and more laughter. Mom was a good cook, and her sewing and knitting talents were exceptional. (*Each of her grandchildren has their own handmade Afghan knitted by "Nan."*) The following summer, I was more mature and agreed to try Girl Scout Camp again. This time I loved swimming, my extra curricular activities, and friends. One morning during breakfast, my best camp friend, Sylvia, happened to glance over at the dining room entrance door and said, "Sissy, isn't that your dad?"

Looking up, I saw a very erect Army officer dressed in shiny boots with a helmet under his arm, wearing aviator- type sunglasses and carrying a swagger stick. He was also carrying a box filled with "goodies"—cookies, pastries, and chocolate, none of which were easily available in wartime.

Apparently, Dad's adjutant, a military officer who acts as an administrative assistant to a senior officer, had read my postcard where I wrote saying I was starving. Everyone suddenly became my friend. The "camp boys" who assisted at the camp, were thrilled when Dad let them ride in his jeep to the front gate.

By 1944, Dad had advanced to the rank of colonel and was stationed at Camp Blanding in Florida, where he was training the Nisei (Japanese American) troops. His battalion was part of the famous 442nd Regiment.

The year 1945 was a turning point in history. Two months after being inaugurated for his fourth term as President, Franklin Delano Roosevelt died in March and was succeeded by Harry S. Truman. In May, Germany's surrender ended the war in Europe, and the United States began to prepare its invasion of Japan.

By now, Dad was no longer comfortable training young soldiers and sending them into battle. He had such high regard for the troops he was training that he wanted to go with them. He got as far as Camp Roberts in San Miguel, California, when the United States detonated two atomic bombs over the Japanese cities of Hiroshima and Nagasaki on August 6. On August 9. Japan surrendered unconditionally, and World War II was finally over.

I was twelve years old when Dad was able to leave his full-time Army post. He was offered a job in the private industry as head of research and development for a large food-chain company based in Manhattan. He traveled to New York City to accept the position and arrange for our move to the Big Apple. While he was away, an upper classmate, who had a crush on my brother Joe, invited me to go flying with her in a small, single-engine Piper Cub airplane.

Mom wrote to Dad asking what he thought of the idea of my

flying around in a little plane. (Telephone calls were prohibitively expensive back then.) But the country hadn't yet recovered from the wartime restrictions, and the mail service was slow. So, when the day for the flight arrived, she had still not heard what Dad thought about this. I begged her to allow me to go, and she green-lighted my adventure.

We took off from a small airport and flew over Gainesville, Florida. As we buzzed my house at low altitude, I could see my mom in the yard waving a dish towel. What I couldn't see was the letter from Dad she clutched in her left hand, saying, "No, I don't think she should do this."

With Dad already in Manhattan and Bob enrolled at Michigan State College, it was just Mom, Joe, and me packing up the house and traveling north to New York. Not wanting to drive the long distance alone, Mom sold the family car and booked us tickets on a train bound for Pennsylvania Station. We had a berth in the sleeper car for brother Joe, plus a compartment that would sleep Mom and me, with me in the upper berth. In the compartment was a sink and toilet, eating space, and comfortable seats that turned into beds.

The train was crowded with returning military men and for many it was standing-room only. Mom spoke to the conductor and requested he give my brother's berth to some deserving soldier. She said my brother could sleep in the upper berth in the compartment, and we girls would share the lower berth. What a disappointment! I had been so excited to sleep in an upper berth. I think I cried and carried on through the whole state of Georgia. *I was scarred for life!*

The move to New York was a big deal for our family, because our new house in Bellerose, a quiet, middle-class neighborhood on the eastern edge of Queens, would be the first home my parents had ever owned. It also meant that our family, after moving from one military complex to another, just might be able to settle down in a home of our own for an extended period of time.

Dad commuted from Bellerose into Manhattan every day. I entered Public School 33 (P.S.33) mid-year as an eighth grader. As the new kid on the block, I was nervous and timid. On one of my first days at P.S. 33, a teacher asked me to read aloud a passage from the textbook about the salmon industry. Reading loudly and quickly and heightened by nervousness, I mispronounced the word "salmon" by sounding the "L." My heavy southern accent didn't help.

When I finished, the teacher said in an unsympathetic tone, "Very good, Susanah. Now would you please translate for us?"

Apparently, the teacher thought his comment about my thick accent was funny, and the class responded with laughs. But I was hurt and humiliated. The incident must have had a deep impact on me, because to this day whenever I am asked to read or speak in public, I get very nervous.

Thankfully, a kindly neighbor came to my aid. She recognized my unfamiliarity with the new situation and insisted that her son, also an eighth grader at P.S. 33, accompany me on the long walk to school. It was about a mile with crossings of two major traffic arteries, Jamaica Avenue and Grand Central Parkway. I was delighted to be helped by the tallest and best-looking boy in eighth grade.

Eager to make friends, I joined the local Girl Scout troop and the "Sub-Deb" club, basically a sorority for teenage girls. But what really helped me win friends was my new friendship with the boy next door. Because he was so handsome, all the girls in school were dying to come over to my house—so they could see and talk to him. I was instantly popular.

We were in our new home for just two months when Dad received a phone call from Washington, D.C., asking him to go to Europe for three months under the Marshall Plan, also known as the European Recovery Plan, to help restore and modernize the agricultural systems of devastated Europe. Dad told them he would talk to his wife and call them back. He accepted the call to duty, of course, but he had to leave for Europe immediately.

In the fall of 1947, I entered Jamaica High School as a freshman. My brother Joe, now a senior, helped guide me. There were no school buses for us. We had to take a public bus to the subway station, board a train for 165th Street, and then walk up a steep hill to the school building. Mom made me a white pleated skirt that I wore with a bulky, white sweater, adorned with my high school Varsity letters.

Girls Varsity

I loved high school. I continued with the Sub-Deb Club, became captain of the swim team, and enjoyed being part of girls Varsity. Socially we had a group of friends. We went everywhere together. The local ice cream shop, called the Sugar Bowl, was a favorite.

One weekend, I went to a church dance. I noticed a cute guy and wondered why he wasn't dancing. Like most teenage boys, dancing was something to be endured. I walked up to him to introduce myself. He was wearing a yellow shirt, so I hinted in my greeting that he might be a little cowardly.

"For that, my dear, you will suffer," he said. And, taking my hand, he led me onto the gymnasium floor. Then, as always, he did not like to dance.

His name was Charles Kuchenbrod. He was three years older than me and was a junior at Newtown High School in neighboring Elmhurst. Even so, we became an item.

Dance, particularly "modern" dance, had long interested me. My love for dancing began when I was in a dance recital in 1938 at just five years old. We began to tap to the first lines of Bing Crosby's hit "You Must Have Been a Beautiful Baby." The music continued, and then the big girls tapped on stage to the last line, "Cause baby, look at you now."

Because we moved so much, I never could take dance lessons. But at Jamaica High School, my interest blossomed. Mrs. Leahy, Chair of the Girls Health Education Department, also had an interest in dance. She made it possible for me to attend a dance class with Charles Weidman, a renowned choreographer and one of the pioneers of modern dance. The class was held on the stage of a Manhattan theater.

A male dancer, very effeminate, showed us to the dressing room, which was located underneath the stage. To my surprise, dancers, both male and female, dressed in the same room. That night when I returned home, I excitedly told Charlie and my dad all about it. The next thing I knew I was engaged.

Years later, I would ask Mom how she permitted me to get engaged when I was seventeen and still in high school. Her reply was, "Dad and I really liked Charlie, and you were quite determined." Yes, I was my mother's daughter!

Because I expected my schedule to be very crowded in my senior year, I decided to take the required fourth-year English Regents course during the summer session. As part of the course, we studied Shakespeare's Romeo and Juliet. I discussed the play with my dad.

Near the end of the semester, our class was taken to a film version of the play. I wrote my term paper about the film, with some insight from my father. But the last paragraph was my own. I suggested the movie would have been better if filmed in color.

When my paper was returned, it had a big "A" posted at the top, with an asterisk. At the bottom of the page, the teacher had written me a note: "*Ah, Susanah, here you break my heart. This play was meant to be bleak and sad."

Thanks to Mom, no one had a senior prom gown like mine! She sewed my prom gown. The material was white organza with two-inch size dots of black velvet. scattered about the strapless dress. On my bare shoulders I wore a black lace cape. Bright red, garnet-colored stones formed a "choker" necklace and I had matching earrings.

Sue at age 17

Graduation was bittersweet. I had enjoyed my years at Jamaica High School, especially my time studying dance under Mrs. Leahy. At the end of the school year, she wrote in my yearbook, "To your career in dance, I wish you good luck." But that was not the path I would follow.

CHAPTER 4

TWENTY YEARS AS HOUSEWIFE AND MOTHER

My two older brothers had gone on to attend Dad's alma mater, Michigan State College, which would officially become known as Michigan State University in 1964. But Dad felt that a girl didn't need a college education to get married and have a family.

He urged me to go to nursing or secretarial school, good jobs for women. But I wanted to save money for my future with Charlie, so I got a job where he worked, at the New York Telephone Company, affectionately known then as "Ma Bell."

Charlie had worked various jobs, including as a delivery driver for Coca-Cola®. When he learned that the New York Telephone Company was hiring, he applied and was hired as a telephone installer. It was considered a good job with many benefits. To save money he lived at home.

Charlie and I wanted to get married. But it was the early 1950s, and the Korean War had started. Our plans changed when we learned that Charlie was being drafted. My father told him we would have to postpone the wedding, because he could not support a wife on a private's pay. He would first have to become an officer. So,

Charlie went to OCS (Officers Candidate School) at Fort Sill in Lawton, Oklahoma.

We were still determined to be wed and, optimistically assuming that Charlie would succeed, we set a date, November 9, 1952, which was just two days after his expected graduation from OCS. He worked very hard at becoming an officer, while I worked on plans for our wedding. It had to be a simple affair in case Charlie didn't pass OCS. If he failed, there would be no marriage, and he would be sent off to war as a private. If he succeeded, there would be a wedding, and Charlie would still be sent off to war, but as a married officer.

We planned to be married in the Dutch Reformed Church in Queens Village. We were able to make contingent plans for our small reception at the beautiful Stewart Manor Country Club. They understood our problem and they were most cooperative.

My mom arranged to have my wedding dress made at a shop in Garden City. They designed a handkerchief-style gown (which showed off my small waist).

My brother Bob had been married in 1950, so I asked his wife Esther, my new sister-in-law, to be my Maid of Honor. She was going to wear her pale blue lace wedding dress for the occasion.

As hoped and prayed for, Charlie graduated on schedule from OCS as a Second Lieutenant and made his way back to Long Island for our wedding, which went off beautifully. Charlie was so handsome in his Army uniform. Years later, looking back at a photograph, with Charlie holding my hand, my smile said it all.

At the reception, Charlie's former supervisor at the telephone company told him, "It is a shame that the Army interfered because you had a fine future with Ma Bell. Look me up when you get back."

Lieutenant Charles W. Kuchenbrod and bride - 1952

We spent our wedding night at the elegant Garden City Hotel on Long Island, followed by a night at the cozy Three Village Inn in Stony Brook, a quaint town in nearby Suffolk County. We then set off on the long drive to Camp Chaffee in western Arkansas, to which Charlie had been sent, pending his assignment either to Europe or to Korea.

There, we secured an apartment and waited for the expected orders for Charlie to be assigned. Four months later, those orders came, and Charlie was sent to Korea to join an artillery unit as a forward observer. When he left, I went back to Bellerose to live with my parents and continue my work at the New York Telephone Company.

My mom and dad taught me a lot while growing up and later when I stayed with them during Charlie's time abroad. As I recall the many experiences my dad and I shared, I recognize how much his actions also influenced me. On reflection, I have come to understand and appreciate that my father often went out of his way to expose me to different experiences.

Sue's dad in 1979

For example, at one point an official from a French railroad company that Dad knew through his Marshall Plan assignment came to New York to visit. I was fortunate to join my parents and the French official for dinner one night in Manhattan. I think my dad might have boasted that I could speak French.

I ordered a breast of guinea hen under glass. The wine was delicious and as I drained my second glass, Dad whispered in my ear, "If you empty your wine glass, it is a sign to the waiter to refill your glass."

When we parted at the end of the evening, our host, being a true gentleman, said, "Mademoiselle, your pronunciation is (smacking his lips) perfect, but the grammar . . . not so much!"

Dad loved history. Perhaps it was my 16th birthday when he invited me to have lunch with him at the famous Fraunces Tavern at 54 Pearl Street in Manhattan. It is named after the Tavern's owner and is noted on the National Registry of Historic Places. George Washington gave his farewell address to his officers there in 1783.

Once seated, the waiter came over and told us the Special of the Day was trout, flown in fresh that morning. I wanted to appear sophisticated, so I ordered the special. I never thought about whether it would be served whole or fileted.

When the plate was placed in front of me, there were some greens on the side and a whole fish, its blank eye staring up at me. Repulsed, I quickly pulled the greens over the head of the fish.

Dad and the waiter were quite amused. Then, the waiter efficiently deboned the trout, removing the head and that staring eye, and to my delight, it was delicious.

Mom was a good cook and taught me to enjoy preparing meals for my family. Her sewing and knitting talents were exceptional. How I wish I had told her how much I respected and loved her. She showed me it is okay to reach out and experience life. We seldom disagreed.

Nevertheless, I do recall one teenage spat that reflects her calm nature and good judgment: "I'm leaving, and I'm NEVER coming back!" I told her one memorable day.

With a flourish, I stomped out of the house and slammed the front door. As I descended the front steps, I heard a knock on the window and thought, "Ah ha! She wants me to come back." Instead, I turned and saw my mother's hand waving goodbye.

Despite that event, she supported me in all my moods. Now I

wonder how she was able to create a home for us, no matter where we were at the time. We had rented five different houses during the time my dad served during World War II.

Sue and her mom, Susannah Herschberger Hoover, in 1983.

She was a special woman, smart, kind, a good homemaker and loving. She guided our family and kept things together for us during the many periods when Dad was in the Army and away from home. She always made us feel like we were "home" no matter where we lived.

The Korean War came to an end on July 28, 1953. Charlie had served for two years in the Army, seven months of which he was a forward observer at the 38th parallel, between North and South Korea. Despite his dangerous assignment, he returned unharmed, arriving on our first wedding anniversary.

Once back in New York, he returned to "Ma Bell" as a telephone installer, and I continued my job, also at the telephone company. We couldn't yet afford to buy a house of our own, but we were saving what we could, mainly out of Charlie's overtime. We soon settled into an apartment in a two-family house in Cambria Heights, Queens.

At Dad's suggestion, Charlie started college at Brooklyn Tech, which meant that he had to forego his overtime. But when I became pregnant, Charlie decided that I would have to stop work when the baby was born. That would mean we would then need his extra overtime money to live on, so he dropped out of college.

At "Ma Bell," Charlie advanced through the ranks, eventually becoming an outside plant engineer. When we knew about a second baby, house hunting became our weekend activity. A misdialed phone number led us to a realtor "way out" in Syosset. After saving for four years, Charlie and I managed to buy a house there.

Syosset was located in Nassau County, Long Island, some twenty-five miles from the hustle and bustle of Queens. There were no subways and very limited bus service. To get to Manhattan you either drove a car or took the Long Island Railroad into Penn Station.

The house had been empty, and the grass almost obscured the "For Sale" sign. But we had found our home. It was a two-bedroom Cape, with garage, basement, hardwood floors and a happily expandable second story. I walked into the backyard, envisioning my children playing there.

The neighbor offered a comment, "If they are asking $15,000 it is a good deal." We split the commission with the agent, and paid $14,200. *(WE did make some improvements, and seventy-two years later I sold the house for $435,00.)*

Our new house was cozy and small. It had a living room, dining room, kitchen, two bedrooms and a bathroom, all on the first floor. There was a second floor, but it was unfinished, showing joists and rafters. Outside there was a nice yard suitable for kids to play in.

My home for sixty years – One Underhill Avenue, Syosset NY

On January 11, 1955, our first child, Cheryl, came along. Linda, our second daughter, was born exactly two years later, on January 6, 1957.

As I grew into my role of wife and mother, the world around me was rapidly changing. That October, Sputnik, the first artificial satellite, owned by the Soviets, was launched into outer space, and so started the Cold War. The fact that the Soviets had achieved their mission fed fears that the U.S. military had fallen behind in developing new technology, intensifying the arms race between the two nations.

On September 30, 1958, our third daughter, Lori, arrived. (Life was busy with three young daughters.) I looked forward to my relief during morning coffee with my neighbors who also had young children.

The year 1960 was a presidential election year. Dwight D. Eisenhower couldn't run again after having completed two terms.

John F. Kennedy and Richard M. Nixon were the presidential candidates. Alaska and Hawaii became states, making a total of fifty states in the union.

That Fall, Charlie and I welcomed our fourth child, Charles W. Jr. It was November 2, 1960, and I was in the maternity section of the Manhasset Medical Center. As I was being wheeled down to the delivery area, I saw "Delivery Room B," which I immediately associated with the word "boy." I insisted on that room.

My labor contractions had slowed, so Dr. Hindman, the obstetrician, and my husband, Charlie, started discussing the upcoming presidential election. When the contractions rapidly increased, I finally got their attention.

"Sue, hold back while I wash my hands," the doctor said.

Of my three other babies, two had been delivered without any sedation. I knew what to do—take rapid, deep breaths.

After the delivery, because I was near-sighted, Dr. Hindman playfully brought the baby up close and said, "Look, another girl."

I could see he was smiling; I could also see it was a boy!

Now that we had a son, we struggled over his name. My husband was Charles W. Kuchenbrod. A nephew had been born the June before; he was named Charles Magnus Kuchenbrod the Second, after my deceased father-in-law. To add a third Charles Kuchenbrod living in Syosset seemed to be confusing, so we sought another name.

Two days went by with no decision, and I was told that if we didn't name him that day, the records would list my son as "Male, Kuchenbrod," and it would take a court order to rename him later.

"After three daughters, aren't you going to name him Junior?" the nurse asked.

I sighed and said, "Yes, I guess we are."

I soon learned that raising a boy was much different than raising girls. Charles fell off the swing set and cracked his collar bone. I was told not to remove the brace; but giving a three-year-old boy a bath while still in the brace was a major challenge.

At another point, he tripped going down our basement stairs and broke his wrist. Before he was five years old, he had also fallen off his bike, hitting his chin requiring stitches to close the gaping wound.

The pediatrician, Dr. Denis, asked me if I had ever seen anyone receive stitches. I had not, so she asked her wonderful, plump, cleaning lady to come into the office to help. The woman just lay prone over Charles while he was stitched up, and he remained perfectly still.

Charles hadn't started school yet when he came in crying one day and said he had fallen off the neighbor's playhouse. There was a gash on his head, so again, off we went to Dr. Denis who luckily lived nearby. She told my boy that he had a choice, a shot or stitches.

He chose the shot. She shaved his head where the cut was open and put a butterfly bandage on. The shot was for tetanus. Because of concern over a possible concussion, the doctor said, "Don't let him go to sleep."

So, we had cookies and a glass of milk. Then my son disclosed that he did not, in fact, fall off the playhouse. He had thrown a hammer up in the air and it came down on his head. A quick phone call to the doctor. She reassured me the treatment would have been the same.

My husband astutely commented that none of our three daughters had ever seen the inside of a hospital or an emergency room — nor had any hurried trips to the doctor. As I said, raising a son was a new and challenging experience.

To accommodate our growing family, Charlie undertook the sizable job of expanding our home. With just two bedrooms, the kids were all sharing one, and Charlie and I had the other, and all five of us shared one bathroom. Charlie wanted to add two bedrooms and a bathroom on the second floor. To make the upstairs livable, he would have to open up the peak at the back of the house and frame in a new roof.

We couldn't afford to hire help, and Charlie had the capacity, so he did all the work himself. He wanted the kids to have their own rooms. It was very important to him. He wanted the best for everybody, me and the kids, for his family.

Because his available time was so limited, and because his excellent craftsmanship made him a perfectionist, we spent a long time completing the construction. He would come home from work in the evenings, have a bite of supper, and go to work on the house. That meant I had to carry the brunt of everything else, the cooking, the housework, the kids, and even mowing the lawn. It was difficult, and the construction went on for a long time.

At one point early in the construction, before the floors were completed and some of the floor joists were still exposed, Charlie mis-stepped and put his foot right through the living room ceiling. Soon after, I arrived home to find my husband sitting on the living room sofa with baby Charles in his arms, wrapped in a little blue blanket surrounded by scraps and dust of sheetrock.

I guess I slowed the construction work down some, too. After the new roof, bedrooms, and interior walls were completed, Charlie asked me to help pick out the plumbing fixtures for the bathroom. I insisted on an off-the-floor, wall-hung toilet. I figured that it would be much easier to clean the floor if the toilet was suspended in the air.

To please me, Charlie agreed, but it required demolishing and reconstructing one wall of the bathroom in order to make it strong enough to carry the suspended toilet. It was grueling work, but Charlie was determined, and he completed the upgrade.

We readily adjusted to the Syosset community. We joined the Community Church of Syosset, an open and affirming congregation of the United Church of Christ. Soon Charlie was elected to be an elder there. I began to play bridge and go bowling with some of the church ladies and I got to know Jean Butler, who was Director of Christian Education at the church.

Charlie continued working hard and was moving up through the ranks in the phone company. I was now caring for four babies born in just a five-year period—all the while settling into, improving, and enjoying our small two-bedroom Cape Cod house, complete with mortgage and perpetually under construction. We were always living on a tight budget. Despite the distractions and tensions, I loved being a mom and life seemed good.

The local Cub Scout program offered our son opportunities to be involved with other boys who were all the same age. The "Pinewood Derby" was a project where each boy received a rectangular shaped piece of balsa wood and was tasked with turning it into some type of racing car. With the help of adults, to compete in the derby they would slowly shape and then paint it. Two nails would hold the two sets of plastic wheels in place. The maximum weight was five ounces.

The two "Charlies" worked very hard, and the end result was amazing. After all the carving and sanding was done, they spray painted the car bright blue, with decal flames on the hood. It was impressive. They added some weight near the rear axle. To be sure the weight didn't exceed the rules, they took it to the post office to be weighed on a sensitive postal scale.

In a proud moment for both father and son, the car won both awards during the competition, one for speed and the other for appearance.

At the end of the Pinewood Derby, the mother of one of the other Scouts turned to my husband and asked, "You aren't going to let him take both prizes, are you?"

"Yes, he earned them," my husband replied.

The December holiday party for the Cub Scouts was held in the elementary school and included separate celebrations for each of the common faiths—and a visit by Santa Claus.

The girls and I sat in the gym, watching the activities. Suddenly the double doors used to enter the gym burst open. With a loud "HO,

HO, HO," Santa Claus appeared with a big belly made from our bedroom pillows.

"Merry Christmas to all," Santa shouted. He wore a bright red suit, whiskers, and had sparkling blue eyes. The girls saw right away that it was their dad; they were half-proud and half-embarrassed.

Cheryl, our oldest daughter, was very nervous when she had to make an oral report in sixth grade. Her dad bought a reel-to-reel tape player so she could tape herself for practice. She practiced so much each family member could have done the report for her. "Although I am not a paleontologist, I do know this..."

Linda, our second oldest, enjoyed dancing, and she was a cheerleader at the junior high school. Charlie depended on her to address our many Christmas cards, because her handwriting was so neat.

One Saturday, Linda was feeling very sad. There was a birthday party she had not been invited to attend. Besides that, her boy of the moment was going to be there. Once again, Charlie came to the rescue, offering up a plan for a family activity. "Come everyone, load up the sleds," he said. "We are going to Bethpage State Park. We will go sleigh riding and then enjoy some hot chocolate."

Linda immediately felt better. Then, as we were loading the car, the "special' boy walked up the driveway towards Linda. She was surprised and asked why he wasn't at the party.

He replied, "When I found out you weren't going to be there, I didn't want to go. I was hoping we could do something together."

The boy was dressed for a party, not sleigh riding, with blue jeans, loafers, and a light jacket. Still, he went sleigh riding with us.

Lori, our third daughter, loved helping her dad no matter what they might be doing together, be it mowing the lawn, washing the car, or raking leaves. Just being with him made her happy.

In December, all the staff at Charlie's workplace invited their children to the office for a party. While at the party, Charlie noticed

Lori had some swelling near her ear—yet another case where Dad was attentive and caring. She felt fine, but he brought the children home.

The pediatrician said it was not the mumps, but something worse. The gland was infected and very difficult to treat. The doctor recommended a warm poultice, made from a clay-like substance. Using the bottom legs of flannel pajamas, I cut strips, spread the warmed poultice on the cloth, then wrapped it with the strips, to hold the poultice in place. She wore it day and night.

Tearfully she asked me if she would have to wear "that rag" around her neck on Christmas.

SUE'S FOUR CHILDREN

Sue's children (l to r) Lori, Linda, Cheryl, Charlie, in 2021

Charlie was a strong man, in many ways. He worked very hard, whether in OCS, at his job, or enlarging our home. He was a chief umpire for the Little League, an Elder at our Church and a kind and helpful neighbor.

In 1969, at age 39, Charlie suffered his first heart attack. It was the year Americans landed on the moon, but they were also in Vietnam. The Sesame Street television program introduced us to Oscar, the

Grouch, who was originally orange. Remember singing *Sugar, Sugar, Days of Aquarius,* and *Let the Sunshine In?* The economy was good and foods like Green Giant frozen peas, frozen bread and ready-to-bake pie crusts were all the rage. A Snickers candy bar, 2.3 ounces, cost ten cents. The 34th President of the States, Dwight D. Eisenhower, died on March 28, 1969, and Charlie had his heart attack one month later.

Charlie couldn't accept that being overweight, drinking martinis, and smoking contributed to his health problems. His reason was it was my nagging. (Indeed, I did nag).

Having a heart attack brought a drastic change in Charlie. In recovery, he lost considerable weight and took pleasure in purchasing a new wardrobe. He also stopped smoking and drinking, and he looked years younger. One of Cheryl's girlfriends commented to Cheryl, "I didn't know you had an older brother."

Although there were other health issues, they were controlled by medications.

Now that the kids were older and in school during the day, to earn a little spending money,I wanted a part-time job that had working hours from 9:00 a.m. to 3 p.m. I searched the local *Pennysaver,* a weekly circular of ads that included a 'Help Wanted' section, hoping to find a listing that met my needs.

One looked promising; World Book Encyclopedias was looking for a local salesperson. I called and scheduled an interview at a nearby diner.

When I was young, my parents purchased the World Book series, *Childcraft: The How and Why Library*. It was a four-book set designed especially for pre-school and primary grade children. I loved reading them. *Was this an omen?*

Growing up, my family moved from one state to another; over seven years from 1939 to 1946, I attended five different schools. This in itself had been an education. Now I was going to sell World Book Encyclopedias.

What most appealed to me was the company's offer of a free set to any salesperson who would make ten house calls. I really wanted a set to help my children get used to researching and looking up answers to their unending questions.

After completing the World Book sales training, I believed this was a good product, but I still balked at the idea of "cold calling" knocking on doors with no appointment. My manager showed me a good sales technique. He agreed cold calling is very difficult, then offered a solution: I didn't have to go house to house. I could "interview" ten people in a week and get a set wage instead of a commission. That was easy, as I could call on my relatives and friends.

Brushing aside my husband's negative view of this new job, I finally made my first call. The sales training was excellent. For instance, once I was in the home and the people were interested, I would suggest that when the books were delivered, they should avoid storing them in the den on a bookcase or in the child's bedroom. Instead, they should find a place near the dining area.

"If, during breakfast, your child asks, 'Why is the sky blue?' you can't call the library, as it isn't open," I'd say. "The best time to answer a question is immediately. So, grab the 'S' volume and get the answer. Other encyclopedias have extensive information, generally far more information than you need, but World Book answers the question and also encourages you to keep on reading," I added.

Once I earned the free set, I lost interest in selling/ Today, we get our information online—from Google, Siri, and the internet. Even the World Book Encyclopedia is available there.

In the fall of 1971, the Administrator of Church Education at our family church, Jean Butler, announced that she would be taking a sabbatical year off from her duties beginning in June 1972, and I was asked to assume the position on a full-time basis. With all four children now in school, I readily agreed to the one-year commitment.

At that time, Mal Bertram was the pastor and Fred Bachman was the associate pastor. Both were very helpful and encouraged me in my work. I loved the work and the meetings with the pastors. It was challenging and a wonderful learning experience.

Confirmation Class with Pastor Bertram on left and Sue on right

That Fall, the church took on an intern, Tom Hunter, a young, hippie-type who was very good with the children, strumming his guitar and singing songs.

We were all excited when we learned that Lori had invited Tom to share Christmas Eve with us. It's not often you get to enjoy live music in your home to ring in the holiday. Life is often filled with unexpected moments of joy, as well as sorrows.

Two days later, we lost our beloved Charlie in the plane crash, and life as we knew it was irrevocably changed. I was still working at the church in December 1972 when Charlie died.

CHAPTER 5

A NEW YEAR & NEW EXPERIENCES

I struggled to overcome the shock of Charlie's death and to figure out how to raise four teenagers and get along without my husband. Thankfully, my brother Bob stepped up to lend a hand. We discussed what matters needed attention. When I told him Charlie did not leave a will, he suggested that now I, too, had to have a will.

A lawyer neighbor named George Tayback offered to come to the house to discuss things. While George was there, a man knocked on the front door. He said he was from Eastern Airlines and needed some information.

In fact, he was a 'scavenger' seeking to get information about the plane crash that he could sell to Eastern. George quickly caught on to his deception and forced the man to admit he was not employed by Eastern.

George's response: "Get the hell out of here!"

Still in shock and bewildered by my sudden loss, I turned to my pastor, Mal Bertram. Mal raised a question about a possible lawsuit and said he would talk to the church attorney for some advice.

Later that day. he called and reported that the church attorney had recommended that I hire Lee Kreindler, an attorney in New York

City who was well known for his successful lawsuits against the airlines.

Further discussion resulted in George Tayback agreeing to do a will for me, but when we asked if he could represent me on my claim against Eastern, he said he could start but we really should retain a lawyer with expertise in aviation law. He, too, thought Lee Kreindler was a good choice.

Cheryl and Linda, our two oldest daughters, celebrated their 18th and 16th birthdays in early January. My parents returned home to Washington, D.C., and it was time for my children to return to school. Their friends and teachers showed them much compassion for the loss of their father.

Cheryl's twelfth grade chemistry teacher hesitated to call me, but decided it was important. He apologized for adding to my worries but said Cheryl was failing chemistry. He knew she wanted to be a nurse and wouldn't be accepted in nursing school without a passing grade.

I really appreciated his call and his candor. I hired a tutor who helped her pass the Chemistry Regents exam, and she earned a good score.

Our son Charles was twelve years old when he lost his dad. I wondered how a boy without a father learns to be a man, not just sexually but in all ways. I discovered that basically he would learn from other men, including his male relatives. Also, from the men that we, his mother and sisters, would eventually date, and from other fathers who included him when they took their sons to sporting events.

That year, Charles had entered the seventh grade at H.B. Thompson Junior High School in Syosset. For the first time, he experienced changing classrooms for different subjects, as well as many social changes, like having more students in his classes and more freedom during the day. The guidance staff and teachers at H.B. Thompson provided support in many ways. They knew my son liked cars, such as our '65 Ford Mustang, so they tried to incorporate topics of interest into his studies.

In math, he was taught how many quarts of oil were needed in a car, that tire pressure was important, how much time was needed to stop a vehicle going at a certain speed, what N. S. E. W. meant and how to use this information. The teachers expected good grades from him and assigned him expanded reading lists. I am so grateful for all the educators, especially in the Syosset school district, those who really care and meet the needs of their students.

After his father's death, people would say to my son, "Now you are the man of the house."

No! I thought. He was a twelve-year-old boy. But he never needed to be reminded that the garbage needed to be put out by the curb, or the lawn needs mowing. He became handy with tools of all kinds and, as his mom, I believed he could do anything.

It was a warm, lovely spring morning. The children had left for school, and I was sitting at the kitchen table, sipping my lukewarm coffee. Reflecting on my changed life, I found it difficult to imagine it without Charlie. Six months had passed since his death, and still, I hadn't fully taken it in.

Half-dreaming, my eyes wandered around the room. One wall was papered with an ivy design that climbed up a trellis. My attention was drawn to the yellow telephone that hung on the wall above the table.

THE TELEPHONE RANG.

A friend of mine who worked at the local public library had reached out to me several days earlier. She knew that the library was seeking part-time clerical help and thought that I would be a great fit for the position. She had hand-delivered the job application to me, waited until I filled it out, and returned it to the library office. I had forgotten all about it.

After a moment of hesitation, I answered the call. It was the library office; they had received my application and wanted to set up a date for a job interview.

Another sip of the now cold coffee and **THE TELEPHONE RANG, AGAIN.**

This time it was a male member of my church asking me for a date. The invitation made me uncomfortable. I had been a widow for only a short time; the idea of dating had not entered my mind. I promised to call him back after checking with my family.

THE TELEPHONE RANG for a third time. It was from the office of Kreindler and Kreindler, the law firm in New York that handled aviation cases. Pastor Mal had asked a church member who was a lawyer for advice, and the man had recommended the firm. Separately, I had also reached out to a neighbor and friend who also happened to pilot a pleasure aircraft during his off hours. He, too, suggested that Kreindler & Kreindler LLP, founded by Harry Kreindler and his son, Lee, in the 1950s, would be the right firm to help me.

The younger Kreindler had been an outspoken opponent of a proposed helipad atop the 808-foot-tall Pan Am building, located on Manhattan's East Side. Despite his concerns, from 1965 to 1968, Pan Am used the rooftop as a helipad to transport passengers to its terminal at J.F.K. airport, resuming its activity in February 1977.

Two months later, on May 16, there was a fatal accident, just as Lee Kreindler had warned. Five people were killed when a rotor broke off a New York Airways Sikorsky S-61 helicopter, causing the aircraft to crash into the window of a nearby skyscraper and a piece of the blade to land on Madison Avenue.

He would also play a role in the prosecution of Trans World Airlines, (TWA), following the crash of Flight 800 off the coast of Long Island in 1996, and lawyers from his firm would be appointed lead counsel for the plaintiffs in nearly every major commercial airline disaster case in the U.S. and abroad.

We arranged a time and date for an interview at his office in New

York City. It had only been four months since Charlie's death, and I was still feeling a bit overwhelmed. I knew I needed guidance when I found myself aimlessly walking around in my backyard.

I called Pastor Mal and explained my morning. As usual, he had sound advice. First, he said, when you have multiple concerns, separate them and deal with them one at a time. He advised me to go to the job interview. "The best way to go on an interview is when it really doesn't matter if you get the job," he stated.

Second, he counseled me on the best way to respond to the invitation from my fellow church member. He told me that the gentleman who called me was also a widower. "If you are not ready to date, just tell him," he advised.

Pastor Mal had advice about that third call, too. "I think I hear you saying you are nervous about going into Manhattan and, yes, I will go with you," he said.

I got the part-time library job, told the widower I wasn't ready to date, and would travel into Manhattan accompanied by Pastor Mal to meet with the lawyer.

In a strange twist, soon after George Tayback completed my will, he unexpectedly died, and his practice was turned over to an associate named Ira Hynes, whom I did not know. Ira called and when he learned of my meeting with Lee Kreindler, he offered to drive Pastor Mal and me into Manhattan, an invitation I graciously accepted.

The morning of the interview with the attorney, while I was nervously dressing, I put my thumbnail through the upper leg of my pantyhose. There was a large hole, but I knew there was no time to change.

Pastor Mal, Ira Hynes and I arrived at the Manhattan office and took the elevator to the top floor. The receptionist smiled, called us by name and said, "Mr. Kreindler is waiting for you." She then ushered us into a spacious office with breathtaking views of the New York City skyline.

Lee Kreindler was seated at his desk. He stood and walked over to introduce himself to the three of us. Two other well-dressed men, associates in the firm, were in the office, too. Mr. Kreindler held a yellow legal pad and pen in his left hand. Moments later, we were seated in front of his desk. He seemed engaged in our conversation and began writing down my answers as we talked. He knew how to make me feel at ease.

After a couple of minutes, he looked up, smiled, and asked me if I would be comfortable with him recording our conversation. I had no problem with him putting everything on tape and so we continued. Later, he suggested that we take a short break.

As I rose to cross the room, I felt a huge run down the side of my pantyhose. *Had any of the men noticed it?*

The receptionist joined us and showed me to the ladies' room. A very pleasant secretary from the office entered the restroom, noticed my distress and asked, "Are you okay?"

"Yes," I said—but went on to share my angst about the large hole in my stocking.

"No problem," she replied, smiling. Returning to her desk, she pulled open a drawer and among many items like hairspray, cosmetics, sewing kit, and nail polish were new packages of pantyhose, and some were my size.

I thanked her profusely, then returned to the ladies' room to change.

Back in the office, Mr. Kreindler spoke of his many experiences in representing people in lawsuits against airlines for damages caused by plane crashes. He felt that his lawsuits had helped the airlines improve their operations. He was also a member of the National Transportation Board. He told me that flying is now the safest way to travel, and we need to keep it that way.

Through all this, Ira Hines, the lawyer who had accompanied us, hadn't said a word. Finally, he interrupted, advising that he had another appointment. Mr. Kreindler remarked that he was confident that Mal and I could find our way to the Long Island Railroad, and Ira left us.

As lunch time approached, Mr. Kreindler suggested that Pastor Mal and I might want to take a walk so we could have some time to talk. But first, there were more questions. The dominant item for discussion was replacing the financial loss that my children and I had incurred as a result of my husband's death.

"How do you put a numerical value on someone's life?" I asked the attorney.

"You cannot," he said. "You can't undo what has happened. The only action possible is to try to discern the loss of financial support in the future, based on previous and projected income. An actuarial table is used, with no emotions involved."

As the pastor and I stood to leave the lawyer's office for lunch, Mr. Kreindler mentioned that, if we found ourselves near a particular restaurant, he recommended we try it.

"Here is that place that was recommended," Mal suggested as we approached the restaurant. "Let's go in."

The place looked expensive, and I worried about how I could pay the bill for the two of us. After all, I had invited the pastor to come with me. I also knew ministers did not make a lot of money. To make matters worse, this was before women had their own credit cards, which meant I would have to pay the bill in cash.

Mal and I talked for a long time. When he finally asked for the check, the waiter replied "Oh, we don't charge you after 3 p.m." Then he smiled and said Mr. Kreindler had called and said that if we happened to come by, "lunch was on him."

What a relief!

There was so much for me to learn. Charlie had handled all the finances and paid the bills. I didn't even know how much he earned. The attorney and the accountant asked me to provide some information to them, but I didn't have any idea where the birth certificates, wedding license, tax bills for the house, and other documents were stored. And because Charlie died with no will; the law would dictate the disbursement of funds.

Because Charlie was on vacation at the time of the plane crash, his death benefits from the New York Telephone Company were limited to one year's salary and one month of free telephone service. There was a $10,000 life insurance policy, too. The phone company representative that I was working with suggested I use it to pay off some of the house mortgage. I simply had too many decisions.

With help, I set up a budget, figured what my income would be and underestimated the expenses. Any money from the lawsuit from Eastern Airlines was not included, as I was told it could take a very long time.

We no longer needed the big station wagon, so I asked my son Charles and his best friend, Steve Goldbaum, to accompany me to the car dealer to buy a Ford Capri, a small two- door coupe.

Talking with the dealer, I thought that the car seemed very small. To set me at ease, the salesman remarked, "Both of your sons fit in the back seat."

Ever since then, Steve has been my other "son," and he remains so to this day.

When my parents arrived for a visit that weekend, the family gleefully told them I had bought a bright yellow sports car.

Still our future was bright. We had so much, family, friends, good health, and each other. I have told friends and relatives to be sure they have a will and be informed about these matters.

Then put them in a safe place and go on living!

CHAPTER 6
JIM

I had never heard of Parents Without Partners, or PWP, until 1974 when Charlie's divorced sister Flo invited me to go bowling with her one evening. It had been two years since Charlie passed, and I needed adult companionship. I decided to give PWP a try. The group was hosting an event at a local bowling alley. Flo and I entered the Westbury Bowl and were immediately hit by the scent of popcorn and beer, and the clatter of pins and the rumble of bowling balls. The lights were bright over the lanes but dim everywhere else.

The PWP group had assigned lanes, and when we arrived, the group welcomed us to bowl with them. Everyone was friendly, and Flo and I promptly joined in. When it was time to leave, they invited us to join them at the local diner for a coffee. I was so naïve that I was surprised to see that people really did go out at that late hour.

One person in the group was a man named Jim Speedling. As we left the diner, he asked us to come bowl with them again on the following Tuesday evening. This was the start of a wonderful relationship, even though Jim was twelve years older than I.

At the time the twelve-year age difference didn't matter. I had found a really special man. He handled the shock of his wife dying from breast cancer by working very hard. He was only in his early fifties and had one son. Like my father and my husband Charlie, Jim had served in the military.

Interestingly, back around 1940 a friend of Jim's convinced him to take two weeks of summer camp by joining the National Guard. That was fine until the Guard was federalized as a result of the war that had broken out in Europe—and suddenly Jim was in the nation's armed forces.

In the Army, they made Jim a lifeguard and stationed him at Breezy Point, on the south-western tip of Long Island. He was working as a lifeguard one Sunday afternoon and when he returned to base, he was told that Pearl Harbor had been bombed. At first, he thought they said Belle Harbor, which was nearby, but then he realized what had actually happened. The bombing was a terrible moment for all Americans, and it suddenly changed the nation's position on that war in Europe.

Jim was sent to combat duty immediately. He seldom talked about his war experiences, but I did learn that he had served in the infantry, fighting all the way from Sicily, through the boot of Italy, up to the Italian border in the Alps. He had many experiences. He saw Mussolini, killed by partisans, hanging upside down in an Italian gas station.

Jim in his army uniform in 1942

Most of his war stories were positive, about the wonderful Italian people and the beautiful country. I knew he had spent time in foxholes, saw buddies killed, and was frightened at times. Most often though, he would praise the Red Cross, the medics, and his fellow soldiers.

Over the years, I learned to play golf with him. We dined at many fine restaurants, and we both enjoyed dancing and traveling. We dated frequently and shared many wonderful trips together. He never complained. In fact, Jim never focused on the negative aspects of life, and he had a kind word for everyone. My life was truly blessed by knowing Jim.

I recall one night we went out to dinner. It happened to be my birthday, but I had not made any mention of it to Jim. After coffee, the waiter brought a small cupcake with a single candle on it and handed it to Jim, asking "Is this what you wanted?"

I was surprised and asked Jim, "How did you know it was my birthday?"

Jim hemmed and hawed and finally mumbled that he had someone check me out at the county clerk's office.

I was outraged! "How dare you check up on me?"

My daughter Lori quickly came to his rescue. "Mom, I told him I didn't think it was fair that Jim did not know. But I made him promise not to tell where he got the information."

My faith in Jim was immediately restored. Jim would not betray Lori, and all was forgiven.

CHAPTER 7

JUGGLING KIDS, A JOB & COLLEGE

By 1975, the Vietnam War had ended. Bill Gates and Paul Allen had created Microsoft, and millions were watching *Saturday Night Live*. The inflation rate was 7.2%, and a new Ford Mustang cost $4,105.00. And I was contemplating going to college.

Pastor Mal Bertram knew I regretted not attending, so he suggested I start now. *What? How could I do that with children, a house to care for, and a part-time job?* Besides, I would be in my late forties before I could finish a two-year associate degree, I reasoned.

Pastor Mal pointed out that I was going to be in my forties whether I attended or not. He was right. In the years since losing Charlie, Mal had been a North Star to me and many others in the community. Under his tutelage, our church's small nursery school grew as did the Sunday School. Mal also started a community senior day care center, joined SCAN (Syosset Concern About Narcotics), was active in local organizations and spent Saturday mornings at the local high school with the various sport teams. They prayed, not to win but to be safe, play fairly and respect one another. Our local rabbi said he would have been there, too, if it weren't his Sabbath.

When the privately-owned Syosset Hospital was rumored to be closing, Mal actively worked to make it a community hospital. He noted when a community starts to lose important facilities, it is beginning to decline. As many of the residents commuted by the LIRR, Mal instituted a morning worship service on the train, as it traveled into Manhattan.

During the 70s, as the anti-war movement gained momentum, students from Syosset High School started a protest march. Their goal was the Kollsman Instrument Inc, a company located on Underhill Blvd. that designed and manufactured aviation instruments. When Mal learned of this, he met the protest group in town and led them to the Church. Who knew what might happen?

One year, Mal ran the New York City Marathon, 26.2 miles through the five boroughs of NYC. On his retirement ,e was "roasted" by the Chamber of Commerce, with more than 100 people in attendance. During this time, he also earned his Doctor of Ministry.

I know of his personal counseling to not only members of the Church, but also to others who benefited from his wisdom. Personally, I experienced his counsel. I once asked him how he was able to accomplish so much. He replied, "If you want it enough, you can make it happen!"

My first class at Nassau Community College in Garden City was English 101. It was an evening class that began at 7 p.m. The professor was excellent. He also taught at Sewanhaka High School in nearby Floral Park. During one class, he shared a story about a student who was in his high-school class. She didn't like school, was tough, and her language would make a truck driver blush.

While studying the opera *Madam Butterfly*, the class read the story and listened to the opera played on a phonograph. For a special experience, the class went to see the Puccini opera live. During the performance, the professor was observing this student, and she seemed indifferent to what was happening on the stage.

When the beautiful Japanese girl learned her lover was returning home and never coming back, she grabbed a sword and killed herself. At this moment, the student jumped up from her seat and shouted, "You son of a bitch!" She had gotten it!

It had been three years since Charlie's death. Cheryl, our eldest daughter, was now attending nursing school. Linda, our next oldest, was graduating from high school. Soon, they would be on their own life journeys. Lori was a high-school sophomore, Charles Jr. was in the eleventh grade, and I was attending college.

Our claim against the airline was settled at the very substantial figure that Mr. Kreindler had worked out. Basically, my financial burden was lightened, but I had no idea how to manage money.

It seemed to me that now was the time for a special vacation. I mentioned Europe but my son Charles queried, "What will we do, look at old cathedrals and museums?"

"Okay, Charlie, where would you like to go?" I asked.

"Hawaii."

I was happy to indulge my son, and everyone seemed excited at the prospect of traveling to Hawaii.

Map of Hawaiian Islands

This would be my first time on a commercial airplane since my flight to Florida to identify my husband's body. It would also be the first time any of my children had been on a plane. They were excited about going to Hawaii. None of us had fears based on Charlie's airplane crash.

For me, Charlie's death was a turning point in so many ways. I'd had to step up and into my husband's shoes and fill the roles of both parent and provider. It had felt an insurmountable task in the beginning, but I surprised even myself with how well I'd risen to the occasion.

We traveled to Hawaii at Easter time, departing from New York's John F. Kennedy International Airport on a 747 airplane. We were in the main cabin for this long trip across five time zones. And, like most passengers, we spent a portion of the time watching a movie. Back then, there was one screen at the front of each cabin, and everyone watched the same film.

When the movie ended, Charles raised the window shade. He looked at me and asked, "Mom, what is that on the ground?"

Looking out the window, I told my son I didn't know what we

were flying over, but a man in a seat nearby introduced himself as Walter and told us it was the Grand Canyon.

We landed in California, where we would board a second flight for the next leg of our trip to Honolulu. As we exited the aircraft, the cockpit door was open, allowing departing passengers to thank the pilot. I was surprised when he invited my children and I to peek in to see the amazing array of instruments. The Boeing 747 was in its heyday, and she was regarded as the Queen of the Skies.

Our tour guide in Hawaii, Bill, a tall, dark-haired and handsome Hawaiian man, was waiting outside the terminal in Honolulu to drive us to our hotel on famous Waikiki Beach. The hotel was new and very modern. We were surprised to see that the elevators were on the outside of the building. The views of the beaches and Diamond Head were breathtaking. The famous, five-star luxury pink hotel, the Royal Hawaiian, was our neighbor. Though we didn't stay there, we did get to enjoy a dinner there.

Meals were included on our tour and each of my children had his or her own money for the special things they wanted to do. The girls went shopping and I visited local sites.

Walter, the man we met on the plane, took Charles on an outrigger canoe and did some guy things with him. I was delighted that my son had this somewhat impromptu male influence on our vacation. It was a wonderful opportunity for someone who was always surrounded by females, doting on him like four mothers.

Our tour included a visit to the "Halona Blow Hole" and Eternity Beach. Our tour guide, Bill, pointed out the site of the torrid love scene from the 1953 blockbuster movie *From Here to Eternity* starring Burt Lancaster and Deborah Kerr. It was a sandy beach sheltered by a large outcrop.

We traveled on a small tour bus, and during the ride, my two eldest daughters, Cheryl and Linda, now twenty and eighteen respectively, told me about their adventure the night before. They had gone to a show, *The Naked Waiter Review*.

Suddenly conversation on the bus stopped, with everyone straining to hear about the show's star, a man named Butch. According to my daughters, Butch was built like the famous Charles Atlas, a body builder from Long Beach, New York, whose friends likened him to the statue of Atlas. Butch's "costume," they said, consisted of an orchid lei and a tiny, white ruffled apron. He titillated the audience with quick flips of his apron, allowing those who were interested to take a peek.

The state of Hawaii, located in the North Pacific, has a total of 132 islands. The major islands are Hawai'i, Maui, Kahoolawe, Lanai, Molokai, Oahu, Kauai and Niihau. On this trip, we visited five of them, Oahu, Maui, Lanai, Kauai and the Big Island of Hawaii.

On Kauai, we visited the Fern Grotto, a fern-covered, lava rock grotto on the south fork of the Wailua River and enjoyed a Wailua River cruise. Our guide serenaded us with the *Hawaiian Wedding Song*, a beautiful, romantic, and popular song for weddings.

I had read James Michener's novel, *Hawaii*, published in 1959, the same year that Hawaii became the 50th State. His book is considered quite accurate, except for the history of the Polynesians; they came from Bora Bora. But much of the historical information about them is mostly folklore.

One evening we enjoyed dinner at the hotel and stayed for the evening activities. The pianist asked if there were any requests. My son turned to me and asked, "I wonder if he can play 'The Entertainer' from the 1973 movie *The Sting*?"

I mentioned to Charles that a request is usually accompanied with money put in the "tip" glass—and he promptly added a dollar to the goblet next to the piano. The pianist looked surprised at receiving a request from a fifteen-year-old boy. but he smiled back at him and played "The Entertainer," along with other tunes from that time period.

My daughters had been shopping and purchased colorful, tight-fitting sarongs to wear. They were advised of the tradition in the

South Pacific of women wearing flowers in their hair. They learned that if a woman puts a flower on the right side of her head, she is available; if she wears it on the left, she is spoken for. The three girls and I all wore flowers on the right side.

After dinner, the girls moved to the dance floor and danced to the hula music, each with a *lei* around her neck. Cheryl's long blond hair swayed as she moved to the rhythmic beat of the drums. Charles leaned close to me and whispered, "I never knew she could move like that."

We both giggled.

During our tour of the Big Island, we saw fields of pineapples, Kona coffee plantations, acres of macadamia nut trees, the black volcanic sand not yet bleached by the sun, and breathtaking sunsets. Our guide promised we would stop at a local store. Our hotel did not yet have its liquor license, so some on the tour wanted to purchase some libations. The five of us looked around and finally decided on drinks and snacks. As we reboarded the bus, we realized we were late and had kept everyone waiting.

As a punishment, I was informed that I could either dance the hula or kiss the driver. I chose to kiss the driver. He was famous for blowing the conch shell in the movie *Blue Hawaii*.

We drove past beaches with bikini-clad girls tanning in the sun. "Many years ago, the missionaries came and clothed our women with muumuu dresses," our guide told us. "Now the haole, a term for non-Hawaiians, have returned and undressed our women."

As we neared the hotel, Charles said, "Mom, let's go home. Two weeks of paradise is enough!"

Perhaps it was, indeed, time to head back to Long Island. After two glorious weeks in Hawaii, we were all ready to hop on a plane and return home.

We spent our final night at a farewell party in our hotel. Hours later, we were at the Honolulu Airport, saying goodbye to our tour guide, Bill, and waiting for the plane to arrive.

"This has been a very different tour," Bill said. "I generally deal with newlyweds or 'nearly-deads,' and **you** show up with four teenagers!"

l to r. Cheryl, Linda. Charles, and Lori - circa 1985

ALOHA!

CHAPTER 8
A FEELING OF ACCOMPLISHMENT

Life was good. I was working part-time for the Syosset Public Library and was close to completing my degree at Nassau Community College. I enjoyed learning, but at one point, I'd grown weary and wanted to quit.

Hearing this, my son Charles said, "Mom, you always told us to finish what you start." He was right. The day I received my degree in the mail, I was filled with a feeling of accomplishment.

By now, Jim and I had been dating almost a year, and I was beginning to wonder if he might propose to me. We had not talked about marriage, but it was on my mind. *Would he ever propose? Would I refuse him?* I strongly felt that I could never love another man.

I talked to my pastor about it, confiding in him my concerns. Mal paused for a moment and then asked me, "How about the love you felt for your first baby?"

"She was wonderful, precious, and I loved her completely," I replied. "So, when your second baby, Linda, arrived you had to take some of that love away from Cheryl and give it to her—right?"

"Oh no! Linda came with her own love," I said.

"And so, it can be with another man."

Here, as with so much of his advice, Pastor Mal was very wise. I have shared that story many times over the years. Indeed, I had time to reflect back on it forty years later when I found a new love, George Pratt, and married him. But I'm getting ahead of myself.

I also had a conversation with a close friend about marrying Jim and ticked off the reasons I had for marrying him: he was kind, had only one grown son, and was financially comfortable (he was in the jewelry business).

My friend blasted me with her response: "If you said you loved this man and wanted to spend the rest of your life with him, I would understand. But you are trying to put a square peg into a round hole."

Jim never did propose. Perhaps he feared I would say no. He kept his home in Westbury and I kept mine in Syosset. Maybe I worried needlessly.

During our time together, Jim and I enjoyed many wonderful trips, including my very first journey outside the United States. At one point, Jim mentioned that he had to make a business trip to Puerto Rico. He suggested that he could arrange to stay over the weekend if I would consider joining him there.

Many thoughts ran through my mind. I wanted to go. I had traveled very little before, and then only with my own family. But what example would I, being unmarried, be setting for my three teenage daughters? I needed to talk to them.

"No way would I approve of any of you to go on such a trip," I told them. "I have been married for twenty years. I am only forty-four years old and am still considered young by some people. Whatever we could do there, could be done right here."

They understood and urged me to go. Everything would be fine, they assured me. *The children were growing up much too quickly.*

I had been working part time, five days a week, so the long

weekend away meant that I would have to reschedule my Monday hours. My supervisor said she could not spare me that day.

Frustrated, I griped to my friend, Elaine, "Then I will just quit."

"Cool down," she advised, "I will work your hours."

I'd made it over that hurdle, but there was another challenge ahead. Cheryl's boyfriend at the time had just received his driver's license, so I asked him to drive me to the airport.

Cheryl was delighted. But my procrastination (perhaps I was not as certain about my decision as I had led myself and my children to believe) and Brian's careful (read slow) driving caused me to miss my flight.

Luckily, I was able to get a seat on the next flight and would be arriving only a few hours later than I expected. I called the Cerromar Beach Hotel, where Jim and I would be staying, and left a message for him that I would be delayed.

A small four-seat plane took me from San Juan International Airport twenty miles east to Cerromar in Dorado. A young couple already occupied the rear seats, so I sat in the seat next to the pilot. He was a one-man operation who stowed the luggage, removed the wheel chocks, jumped into the pilot seat, started the engine, checked the flight map, and helped us off the at the other end of our short jaunt.

The flight was exciting. I noticed in the distance a large, threatening storm cloud with flashes of lightning, and kept looking for an airport below. All I saw were treetops. Then a small, paved landing strip appeared, and we made it to the ground safely.

My flight mates assumed that I was the pilot's girlfriend because I was in the co-pilot's seat. They were surprised when I joined them on the transport to the hotel. It was a short ride on a dirt road that wove its way through towering trees. At the entrance to the hotel, low palmetto palms with their shaped leaves waved hello, and the sweet scent of jasmine wafted through the air. A sound like "ko-kee" filled the air. I later learned that the sound was made by male KoKee frogs that make this sound to attract a female. "(Kokee" means "free toes" because they don't have web feet).

I entered through a vine-covered walkway and saw the front desk. The front desk clerk searched the files and finally informed me that there was no listing for a guest named Jim Speedling. I was shocked and bewildered and wondered what to do. I asked if I might leave my suitcase at the desk. A line from a Laurel and Hardy show floated into my brain, "Here's a nice mess you've gotten yourself into."

Clad in my new outfit, tight fitting, Burgundy-colored, tie-dyed, bell-bottomed pants and a jacket, I walked toward the cocktail lounge. *Funny, the ko-kee calls made me wonder what I was doing there.* Then I heard my name called and turned to see Jim and his friend, Pete.

Jim explained that when he learned that I would be delayed, he and Pete decided they would play a fast nine holes of golf. We later learned that if you had already registered, your name was placed in a different file than the one for newly-arriving guests.

"All Jim could talk about was how smart Sue is, but he never said how pretty you are," Pete said. *Flattery will get you everywhere!*

We enjoyed dinner at the hotel, and Pete stayed over so he could drive us around Old San Juan the next day. We saw the old citadel Castillo San Felipe del Morro, the tropical rain forest with very tall palms lining a path, a busy shopping area where I bought a wire sculpture, and then had dinner at the El Convento Restaurant in Old San Juan, which was part of the centuries old Hotel El Convento. The building was a former Carmelite convent. Construction on the ornate structure had begun in 1646 under King Phillip IV of Spain. When I visited, it was a fine dining restaurant in an exquisite, old-world setting.

I ordered Spanish paella before Jim and Pete put in their orders.

"Let Sue pick the wine," Pete suggested.

The sommelier had me taste several wines. I hesitated to decide.

so then, with much charm, he suggested what wine would be appropriate for each of the dinners we had ordered.

We returned to the Cerromar resort later that evening and said goodbye to Pete. From the balcony we could see bright blue water through the colorful foliage that beckoned us. We certainly enjoyed the tropical warmth of the setting that felt so different from Long Island.

CHAPTER 9
BERMUDA

I enjoyed dating Jim. He had a lot of patience when teaching me to play golf and would regularly encourage me by complimenting my swing. It was always, "That was a good swing." Kiddingly, he might add, "Next time try hitting the ball."

But as time passed, I realized I was single, and I could go out with anyone who asked me. My daughter's driver-education teacher said he would teach my sister-in-law Flo and I how to do the line "hustle" dance. In the early '70s a disco song by Van McCoy's, "the Hustle" started a flashy, dynamic style of dancing, and I decided to get some dance lessons so I could do it, too. I invited Jim, my family, and anyone interested in learning this dance to come and be part of the class.

Only a few years before this, the limbo dance craze had swept America. "How low can you go" was part of the chant. Sometimes, even my husband Charlie would participate in this dance at a party.

After the dance lesson, Jim sensed that I needed to date others. "Sue, I am going to ask someone else out for dinner," he said. "You go and find out what the single world is all about."

THE PHONE RANG.

When I picked it up, my friend Laurie said, "Hey, Sue, there's a singles bar, the Hidden Barn, right in our neighborhood. Let's give it a try." Laurie was younger than I, divorced, and also attending Nassau Community College.

"Sure," I told her. And off we went. (Ah, reminiscences of early dating as a 40-plus year old widow!)

Music and laughter greeted us as we entered the bar. It was crowded, but I found a seat against the wall and watched the scene as I sipped my wine. It reminded me of a film I had seen in high school about the mating habits of the Great Blue Herons. They don't mate for life but have elaborate courtship rituals. They put their heads down, indicating they are interested in mating. They dance around each other and bob their heads, just like the couples in front of me.

A tall, nice-looking man introduced himself as 'Arped," then asked me why I was smiling. We started to talk. He was much younger, had a ten-year-old son in California, and was divorced.

Laurie had already left with someone.

I excused myself and started for the door. "Wait," he shouted after me. "Won't you have dinner with me tomorrow night?"

Mmmm, why not? I thought. I had been told to never give my address to any stranger. So, I suggested I meet him at Mario's Restaurant near my home.

"I would really like to meet your family," he said.

I finally agreed that he could pick me up at 6:30, and I gave him my address. My family had decided to surprise me and clean the wall-to-wall kitchen carpet in my house. So, while I was at work, they moved all the furniture into the living room. In addition, there was a leak in the upstairs bathroom. The plumber had advised shutting the water off at the main source in the basement until he could get there that night.

My plan was to have the family wave hello and I would scoot out the door and jump into his car. But no. Arped quickly got out of his car, and carrying a bouquet of flowers, he came in the front door, which opened directly into the living room. (Picture the living room full of kitchen furniture.)

My daughter went to get a vase for the flowers, and we heard from the kitchen, "Oh, I forgot, we have no water." *My date was off to a great start.*

We set off for the restaurant. The traffic light was red. Arped stopped, then proceeded to turn right. I asked if they could turn right on red in California. His answer was yes. I then told him that was not the law in New York. It had started to rain so when we arrived at the restaurant, he opened a small, foldable umbrella and escorted me to the door. Then he shook the umbrella and carefully refolded it, pleat by pleat. *I had thought my husband was a perfectionist, but this was too much!*

Arped had an interesting background. Before World War II, his father was a minor official in the Transylvania section of Romania. As the Nazis started to take control of the country, his father was able to send Arped out of Europe. He became an engineer and settled in California to work. He married a beautiful "Californian" girl, and they had a son. His dad had died during the war, but after the war Arped was able to bring his mom to the United States. However, his wife and his mother were not compatible, and the tension was affecting his son, so he and his wife divorced.

I told Arped I didn't know that Transylvania was a real place. He smiled and said many Americans did not realize that. He explained that the book *Dracula*, written by Bram Stoker in 1897, had been inspired by Transylvanian folklore and history. He also mentioned that Count Dracula had been a real person, aka "Vlad the Impaler." Vlad was reputed to be brutal and sadistic. He also had an aversion to sunlight, which led to the vampire legend made popular by Bela Lugosi in the Dracula movies.

Arped returned home to California. Not long after, he wrote to me telling me he wanted to see me again the next time he visited Grumman Company for work. I responded that there were too many hurdles; an east coast/west coast relationship, the age and cultural differences, and very little in common. He wrote back that my letter had saddened him, and he suggested I read *The Little Prince* by Antoine de Saint-Exupery.

I never did.

I think that Arped just wanted some place to visit when he was on the East Coast.

After a few months of "dating" I called Jim. and he suggested, "Maybe we could play around"—laughing and making it clear that he was referring to golf.

The two of us shared many wonderful days of golf on various local courses. Then we decided to go to Bermuda and play golf there. The island was a quick plane trip away, and its courses are renowned for their beauty. Jim arranged for us to stay in a lovely small, English resort near the golf course.

I insisted on paying my part, and all arrangements included my full, married name. From our hillside suite, we could see Bermuda's beautiful turquoise water and blue skies. To our left, and slightly above us, was one of the golf greens.

Scooters are the most common way to get around Bermuda We rented two of them because I insisted; I wasn't riding on the back of Jim's. Once the helmets were fitted and the straps tightened, we rode to the other end of the island. It was very different driving on the left side of the road, especially at a "roundabout," or traffic circle. As I navigated around the first circle, the bike leaned a bit, and I singed my ankle on the hot exhaust pipe.

Scooter like the one that threw Sue to the ground

Bermuda is about twenty miles long and our destination was the bustling capital city of Hamilton. After lunch at a waterfront restaurant, we headed back toward the resort where we were staying. Jim went ahead as I was a little pokey, looking at the scenery. There are very few curbs along the road, but I found one. Off to my left, I spied a beautiful Poinciana tree. The next thing I knew, I was flying over the scooter's handlebars. I hit the ground with my left knee and arm. Stunned, I was grateful when others stopped to help and called an ambulance. Jim soon realized I wasn't behind him and turned around. He saw a large crowd and initially assumed that I had stopped to help someone else—only to discover that the worst had happened.

At the hospital, the emergency room nurse said I had to remove my hand from the wound, so that she and the doctors could examine it.

"It isn't pretty," I said.

"Honey, I can't help you if you won't let me see it."

The nurse cleaned away the dirt and sand and transferred me to the operating room where a doctor stitched the open wound. Fortunately, there were no broken bones.

I emerged from the operating room with a firm type of gauze covering the large open wounds on my arm and leg. It aided in healing and the scars proved to be minimal. Now in a full leg cast, with an opening in the knee area, I was transported back to our resort where Jim asked if I wanted to cut the trip short and go home. I declined because the resort was very comfortable and already paid for.

Everyone was very kind. Meals were brought to the room, and I encouraged Jim to see Bermuda for both of us. The previous evening, I wanted to eat dinner in the dining room. I wore my new palazzo pants with an extremely wide leg that flared out from the waist. As we entered the dining room, the hostess kindly inquired how I was feeling. When she thought I was out of earshot I heard her say, "No, just another guest with road rash."

The unfortunate reality is that tourists in Bermuda often get injured on motor bikes; the traffic is challenging and driving on the "wrong" side of the road makes things even worse.

At the airport, I viewed with dismay, but somehow managed to climb up the long flight of stairs from the tarmac to the door of the airplane. The flight attendant brought me some aspirin.

Back home at JFK Airport, we were the last ones to exit the plane. The crew used a wheelchair to transport me to the waiting room area. My family was beginning to wonder what was taking so long, and then through the doors I appeared.

My friend from work stopped by that evening with some flowers and was shocked to see my condition. Later, the phone rang, and a male voice asked, "Mrs. Kuchenbrod?"

I answered "yes," and he said in a very British accent, "This is the Bermuda tourist department. We understand you left some of your skin on our sidewalk."

It was my friend's significant other. He worked for CBS-TV and was a master at accents and practical jokes. Initially, the orthopedic doctor was worried about my recovery and the stiffness in my leg. But after much effort, I was able to lift my leg a tiny bit. Physical therapy and much exercise helped. I felt I was doing well but my nurse daughter told me I was still limping—which meant even more physical therapy and special leg exercises.

I was fortunate to return to Bermuda several times, but you can be sure I never even looked at, or rode, a "scooter." Taxis or even rental cars are the way to go.

While waiting for my "road rash" to heal, I read a new cycling magazine. I was reminded that in addition to being an enjoyable way to pass the time, bike riding was an excellent exercise to strengthen knees. I probably shared this insight with my family—who, on my next birthday, surprised me with the gift of a three-speed bike.

I cycled everywhere. I used the bike for my daily commute to work, and on weekends I sought out new bike paths for pedaling. The Jones Beach bike path, starting in Wantagh, was a particular favorite. It was safe, it took you across several bridges, and in the "off" season you could even ride on the beach's boardwalk.

In a winter issue of the bicycling magazine, I read about a bike tour in Florida that sounded intriguing. The tour started in Marathon just outside of Miami, and traveling entirely on U.S. Route 1, ended in Key West, more than fifty miles to the south and west. Route 1 is a federal highway that extends for 2,390 miles, starting in Fort Kent, Maine and ending at Mile 0, in Key West. The Florida section alone is 545 miles long.

I knew that early spring would be lovely in Florida, so I made the necessary arrangements and soon set off, alone, to meet the challenge. I met my assigned female roommate and the others from the tour in a motel in Marathon. She was a Canadian and a musician, and I was impressed to learn she had done bike trips in Europe.

Her custom-built bike was designed to be easily disassembled and packed into a suitcase for travel, with the parts carefully packed in order. She explained that all she had to do on arriving at a new location was re-assemble it. To demonstrate, she reached for and opened the suitcase. A tangled mess of tools, parts and pieces of a bicycle fell out.

Apparently, while going through customs at Miami airport, the inspectors had dumped out the neatly packed contents of the suitcase, and finding no contraband, just dumped everything back into the suitcase—including all the loose metric tools that were needed to re-assemble the bike. With the help of our tour guides and a friendly bike group, they were able to sort out the tangled mess and my roommate was ready to start the next morning.

The plan was to eat an early breakfast, cycle for an hour or so, have a coffee break, and continue riding until lunchtime. The temperature was perfect, and there was lots of sun and a gentle breeze at our back. About 4 p.m., we found our lodging for the night and rested before dinner. There, we discussed the ride ahead the next day, which was to include a trip over the Seven Mile Bridge.

Seven Mile Bridge in Florida Keys

Route 1 had two paved traffic lanes, one heading northeast and the other southwest. It is bordered on each side with a narrow, paved "path" and low railings. As we traveled along on the path, I learned to love the big trucks.

When they passed me, they produced a "slipstream" that pulled me and the bike forward. The path was wide enough for a walker or a bike, or emergency repairs, but was also littered with broken seashells caused by seagulls that would drop clams to crack them open. Then they would swoop down to eat the treat inside. The danger was that those jagged pieces of shells could puncture a bike tire, and so we tried our best to avoid them.

Accompanying us on the tour was a "sag wagon," a multi-purpose vehicle that could offer a ride, provide spare parts, and solve minor problems. It was also a "chuck wagon," serving great picnics at deserted beaches along the way.

Clutching the bike's handgrips on the second day, I was glad to see the end of the Seven Mile Bridge was in view. Suddenly, my right calf muscle cramped, and I couldn't use that leg.

But I managed to pedal with just the left leg to reach the next rest area, where everyone was gathered in the covered outdoor picnic area and waiting for lunch. With rest, ice applications, pain ointment and stretching, I was able to make it to our next hotel stop where we called it a day.

My roommate was deaf, and she had told me that once she had removed her hearing aids, I could make all the noise I wanted in our room, and it wouldn't bother her. The hot water shower helped with the leg cramp, and I hobbled to the bed. As I raised my right leg to get into bed, there was a loud cracking noise.

My "deaf" roommate popped up and said, "Was that your leg?"

Nodding yes, I flopped onto the bed and soon found that the pain had vanished, and I could use that leg.

The next day, when I told our tour guide, with feeling, about the cracking noise, he smiled and said, "I am a professor of anatomy, and I suspected you had pulled a ligament." Shyly he added, "I would have pulled your leg myself if I had known you better."

In Key West, author Ernest Hemingway's home was fascinating, and you could get a sense of the type of person he was from the way in which the home was furnished. I found it interesting that many cats live at this house, and some have six toes. Hemingway had named the cats after famous people; in his will, he had provided for their maintenance in the home.

President Truman's little white house was also in Key West, now an interesting museum. I also have been to the Truman Library in Independence, Missouri. When I read the official letters and other material about his presidency, I felt I had gained insight into the man who had to decide to use the atomic bomb. It was a military decision that saved many lives, not only American, but also Japanese.

Looking back, I have been fortunate to be able to travel. Before I went on each trip, I enjoyed researching and learning about the places I planned to visit.

CHAPTER 10
FREQUENT FLIER

Five years had passed since we lost Charlie in the plane crash. Unbeknownst to me, his death would send me in a direction I could never have fathomed. Before his passing, I had only been on a commercial plane once in my life; it was a domestic flight to Michigan to attend a cousin's wedding. I was becoming a frequent flier. I had traveled to Hawaii, Puerto Rico, and Bermuda, and I'd biked around Florida. Now, I was heading to Europe.

My friend Dory's husband, Dick, had an interesting job with CBS News. I enjoyed hearing about his experiences. Dick was assigned to cover the 1977 Silver Jubilee in London marking the 25th Anniversary of Queen Elizabeth's accession to the throne. Dory was going to London, too, and she suggested that Jim and I join them.

We saw many of the important sights. We also went shopping. Jim bought some Cuban cigars at the famous Davidoff Cigar store, while I shopped at Harrods department store. I finally decided to purchase a black cashmere sweater. Then, off to France.

From Dover to Calais in a Hovercraft

The HoverCraft was our transportation for crossing the English Channel from Dover, England, to Calais, France. At Customs the agent asked to see the purchased cashmere sweater. I had the receipt, but they wanted to see the sweater itself, which was packed in the suitcase already being loaded onto the ship. They let me pass.

As the engines powered up, the "boat" rose off the sandy beach and began to glide over the water on a cushion of air. It was an overcast day with some small waves. The ride was very smooth until we experienced a bump. The captain turned on the ship's speaker system and apologized, "Sorry, we just went over a small sailboat." He then laughed and added," I am only kidding." As the weather cleared, we were able to see the white cliffs of Dover disappearing behind us. Next stop France.

Paris is about 300 miles from Calais. We enjoyed dinner at a recommended outdoor café with a view of the Arc de Triomphe. I discovered Paris was everything, even more than I expected. Who couldn't appreciate the Eiffel Tower, Louvre Museum, Notre Dame Cathedral?

It was a lovely spring-like day. As we walked through the Rodin Museum and garden, the bronze statue of "The Thinker," a large male figure, sitting with his chin resting on his bent hand, seemed to be in deep thought. It made me pause. *I wondered what life is really about!* Another memorable surprise was a ¼ scale model of the Statue of Liberty, located on an island in the Seine River.

One evening we enjoyed dinner and a type of Folies Bergère show, and yes, the female performers still danced with bare breasts, a la the cabaret Moulin Rouge. The next day, after a delicious, herbed-spiced chicken dinner, we left the small restaurant and walked a little uphill, to visit Sacre Coeur (Sacred Heart) Cathedral at Montmartre.

In the outside courtyard was an art show. I was fully involved with the sights. Jim was leaning against the wall of the Cathedral, smoking his cigar. He loudly shouted out my name, "SUE!" which made me turn towards him. I saw a man, shabbily dressed in dark clothes, reaching for my purse. In another second my purse would have disappeared into the crowd.

My dad had spoken of Versailles, the hall of mirrors and the signing of the Treaty of Versailles that officially ended World War I. We wished we had more time but knowing Ireland was our next stop made it easier to leave.

It was a short ride from the airport in Dublin to our castle (hotel) golf course and resort. Jim played nine holes of golf while I swam in a beautiful pool, then enjoyed ten minutes in the steam room followed by a relaxing massage. In our bathroom, the towel bars were heated, there was an appliance that steamed a crease into your trousers, and heat lamps were there to help you dry off more comfortably. Real luxury.

Dinner was served in a large dining room, complete with tapestries, wall sconces, candelabra, and soft music. It was chilly in the room where we ate, and I was happy to have my black cashmere sweater. As we walked to the elevator, I realized I had left the sweater on the back of my chair. I quickly returned to the dining room, but my new sweater was gone!

In Dublin, our hotel was located in the center of the city. We had been scheduled to stay in a brand new hotel, but it wasn't completed, so we had to settle for the Grand Hotel. It was convenient; we could easily walk to many of the points of interest. My interest was the Trinity College Library.

The tour company apologized to each of us for the change in hotels with a gift of Waterford crystal toasting goblets. I thought I wanted to kiss the Blarney Stone until I was told you had to lie on your back, tip your head way back and, while someone holds you, attempt to kiss the rock behind you. It didn't look all that clean either, so I passed. The ordeal of climbing small circular stairs in the tower, worn uneven by many shoes, was enough.

We boarded a small bus to take a beautiful drive around the "Ring of Kerry," a scenic drive in southwest Ireland. The driver signaled he was turning, and we drove into a parking area. There was a small Irish-type farmhouse and barn that had pens of different types of sheep in several sizes and colors. Our host on the farm was dressed in an ivory-colored Irish knit sweater, and a paddy cap.

As the group gathered, he suggested we look up to the left side of a large field. Sheep were grazing in a pasture that gently sloped downward. A Border Collie was by his side. With no sound or hand motion, the dog ran forward.

The herder said he was going to instruct the dog to move the sheep down the hill and into the right corner. The dog barked once, wagged his tail and headed up the hill. He circled the sheep, barking, and they moved down and to the right. This task was repeated, moving other sheep to other places. Then the dog returned to his owner's side, sat, and looked up and waited.

"Oh, he's looking for a treat," I said.

"No treat, he's a working dog," the owner sternly replied, adding, "Tonight I might let him sit by me at the fireplace."

CHAPTER 11
MY EVER-EXPANDING FAMILY

How quickly the time flew by. During the passing years, all my children were married and became busy with their own lives. Through the settlement with Eastern Airlines, each of my children had been awarded a sum of money that was intended as compensation for support they had lost as a result of their father's death. Among other things, that included weddings. So, I could really enjoy sharing, rather than dictating their decisions.

As my children found their mates, their weddings were for me a time for sharing. All three of my daughters were married at the Community Church in Syosset. Pastor Mal insisted not only on premarital counseling but also that they wrote and memorized their own wedding vows.

Soon after Charlie died, Cheryl attended nursing school and then began working at a hospital in NYC. She commuted on the LIRR from Syosset to Manhattan. Frequently she would meet Jim when he boarded the train in Westbury. Fortunately, my kids all liked Jim, and although we never married, they considered him like family. To Cheryl he became not only a counselor and father figure, but also a friend. Once, when he was recovering from knee surgery, she posed as his nurse and took him outside his hospital in a wheelchair so he could smoke a cigar. To this day, she has been his "angel," making sure in his declining years that he receives good care.

Cheryl met and married Chris Reisert in 1979. In addition to Mal's premarital counseling, they were blessed to also attend pre-Cana at Chris's Saint Edwards Church in Syosset. Cheryl and Chris have two children, Sarah and Matthew.

Linda, my second eldest daughter, graduated from Adelphi and took a job with Air Contact, a commercial air-freight company, in New York City. She was soon transferred to Tampa, Florida, where she met and fell in love with Sam McClure.

They agreed to have their wedding back here in Syosset, so most of her wedding planning was done long-distance from Tampa. One day she called me, sounding somewhat distraught. She felt she could not choose one of her sisters over the other to be her Maid of Honor, so she asked me to serve instead as Matron of Honor. I was thrilled and honored.

Sam's family came from Florida for the wedding festivities in 1984. I can still visualize Linda de-planing at Long Island's MacArthur Islip airport. Behind her came Sam with her wedding gown, slung over his shoulder, encased in thin plastic and flapping in the breeze. Linda and Sam have one son, Lawrence.

Lori, my third daughter, graduated from Katharine Gibbs School and started working as a hostess in a local restaurant. She began dating Dennis, but then became attracted to Dennis' brother-in-law, Nick Greco. Nick was twelve years older than she and in the midst of a divorce.

When Lori told me she planned to marry Nick, I objected and, for the first time, I refused to meet one of my children's friends. I just felt it was wrong! Lori and Nick went for counseling to Mal, who suggested that Lori and I meet with him. During the meeting, I told Mal why I thought the union was wrong. "It has nothing to do with Nick, it was just the situation," I explained.

Mal's reply: "Sue, Lori is in love with Nick, not a situation." He suggested that I meet with Nick and explain how I felt. Jim made a dinner reservation for the four of us, and we talked. Nick tried to explain his divorce, saying, "I just walked away from everything, the house, our car, her family..."

"What! Were you crazy?!" our waitress interrupted. Having overheard Nick's explanation, I guess she, too, was taken aback and had blurted out her response for all to hear.

Lori and Nick had a lovely wedding on June 14, 1980. Mal performed the ceremony. My reservations about this marriage turned out to be all wrong. Lori and Nick have been happily married for forty-three years. They have had two children, Nicholas and Jessica.

Charles, my only son, received the largest share of the Eastern Airlines settlement, and when he learned at age eighteen that he had full control of the money, he indulged himself for a few years. In addition to entertaining many girlfriends, he bought his share of "boy toys," a motorcycle (*yes, I did ride with him as he went to get his motorcycle license*), and a gun, for which he was licensed. He maintained several cars, including a "Firebird" (similar to the Mustang), and tried out learning to be a private pilot. With some nagging from me, he even graduated from Nassau Community College with an associate's degree.

When he bought a power boat, I insisted he take the Coast Guard training course. He passed with the highest score in the class. I had a hitch welded to the back of our station wagon, and I would tow the boat to the Oyster Bay marina for him.

I'm sure there were incidents I never heard about, but Charles could really accomplish whatever he wanted to learn. When Ursula Spitzer became **the** girl, I was thrilled. She loved him so much but maintained her own style and independence. His friend, Steve Goldbaum (my "other son") advised him he would be crazy to let this girl go!

Their wedding reception was at the Jones Beach restaurant in 1987. Like his father, Charles didn't like to dance, but I do remember I felt I deserved a special dance with my son. I enjoyed every moment of that day. Charles and Ursula have two children, Tyler and Jessica.

I remained in my marital home in Syosset and was working full time as Supervisor of the Circulation Department at the Syosset Public Library. We had a wonderful book discussion group, generally with dinner provided by the hostess. We all worked full-time and many in the group were either library directors or department heads.

My friends and I played bridge once a week. But if anyone wanted to share a problem, we would always put down our cards, to listen and even make suggestions. During this period, I was still attending Nassau Community college part-time and dating Jim. I remember one night, stopping by his house in Westbury after class. He had bought me a sandwich from the deli and made me a cup of tea. I knew then he really cared for me.

Sue and Jim

In July 1986, Jim and I headed for Egypt and Greece. We first landed in Rome, Italy, and then connected with a flight for Cairo. As we exited the plane down the metal steps onto the Egyptian tarmac, we saw our path to the terminal lined on both sides by armed soldiers.

In February 1986, violent protests had begun about a possible extension of compulsory military service from three to four years. The sites the protesters chose were mainly tourist areas, which the government now carefully protected. In all my travels, Egypt was the only country where I needed a visa to enter.

Our hotel was conveniently situated. The first night we could see in the distance the illuminated Giza Pyramid from our hotel window. After dinner, we took a short walk to a "sight and sound" show, with the pyramid as a backdrop. Seduced by jet lag and a glass of wine with dinner, I promptly fell asleep. Jim later remarked, "Here you were, able to view ancient history where it actually occurred, and you were sleeping through it."

I didn't sleep, however, when we visited the nearby palace where Hatshepsut, one of Egypt's three female pharaohs, had reigned thousands of years ago. Our guide helped us pronounce her name by pointing first to his "hat" and then his "cheap suit." Then he praised her vision in starting the building program for the temple Karmic. He also mentioned that efforts had been made to erase her name from history because some people thought that pharaohs should be male.

I had read about her in a book my dad had given me years before. My father was a voracious reader, and one book he recommended when I was a teen was Mika Waltari's *The Egyptian*. The novel is known for its high level of historical accuracy about Egyptian life and culture of the period 2000 BC to 1700 BC. Now, forty years after I read that book, I finally stood in front of the Egyptian palace where the successful female Pharaoh, Hatshepsut, once lived and ruled.

The next morning, we made our way towards the camel stables to get our transportation to the Giza Pyramid. We were warned the guides were crafty. They knew how to operate any camera. Immediately the guide led Jim's and my camels together. even though we had walked in separately. He then asked for my camera and took our picture.

We were warned that we would be offered a ride into the Sahara Desert, and it would be inexpensive. But the down part, the return trip, would be very costly. Also, if you declined the offer, they would try to hurry you through the rest of your visit.

When planning our trip to Egypt, I told myself there were two things I was not going to do: enter the Giza pyramid, and purchase a touristy gold cartouche, with my name spelled out in hieroglyphics. Cartouches were originally reserved for monarchs.

When we got to the Giza Pyramid, we waited until the camels knelt so we could dismount. Being curious I went up to the entrance of the pyramid and leaned over to see what was inside. A man in a *galabiya* (a loose fitting, ankle-length robe) motioned me to enter. The next thing I knew I was on an upward-sloping walkway. Its four and one-half foot high ceiling made me stoop over in order to climb up the ramp. The area at the top held, disappointingly, an empty sarcophagus. Descending on the sloped ramp was even more stressful.

We saw many of Egypt's historic sites and took a dinner cruise on the Nile River. Dinner and entertainment included a talented belly dancer who performed with a three-level candelabra adorning her head. Jim never noticed her candelabra.

On the sleeper train that took us up the Nile Valley, destination Luxor, we went to the dining car for dinner. Our drinks were delivered by a waiter, who placed the drinks on his head and belly-danced his way to our table, not spilling a drop.

Train from Cairo to Luxor in Egypt

Our compartment was in the first car, directly behind the engine. Jim gallantly offered the upper berth, reminding me that the frustration I had experienced on the train with my mother and brother many years ago could now be relieved. So, at last, I got to sleep in an upper berth!

During the night I heard swishing noises, then the train would slow to almost a stop. Soon it would slowly increase speed, only to slow down again with more swishing sounds.

"Why?" I asked Jim in the morning, suggesting that we could be in a sirocco-wind sandstorm. Jim smiled and casually opened the small vertical blinds on the window, revealing bright sunshine and palm trees waving in the breeze.

The train had been stopping and backing up during the night while it was delivering mail, supplies, etc. to the many small villages along the route. In our compartment right behind the engine the swishing noise was made by steam being released from the engine. Luxor's sights conjured up more visions of ancient Egyptian life. I asked where I might buy some frankincense and myrrh incense. I was thinking of next Christmas at home.

We found the marketplace, a very busy, hustling, noisy, aromatic, confusing, exciting scene. While waiting at the "spice" booth, a distinguished-looking English gentleman wearing a small mustache, touched Jim on the shoulder and indicated that aphrodisiacs were displayed on the top shelf. He made a circle with his thumb and forefinger.

Jim smiled at him and said, "No thanks, I don't need it."

We took a replica of a felucca (small wooden boat with a canvas sail) to cross the Nile River. On the western bank was the Valley of the Tombs and our destination, Luxor -Tutankhamen's burial site. I am glad now for my memories of Egypt, even the memory of going into the Giza Pyramid. And I still wear the gold cartouche that I purchased. It has "Sue" on one side and hieroglyphic symbols of my name on the other.

After the Valley of the Tombs, we next boarded a plane for the short flight to Athens, Greece. *The ride was like jumping from a hot sandy beach into the cool waters of the ocean. Both are delightful in their own way.*

In Athens, I marveled at the historic sights, was overwhelmed by, and frankly was unable to fully understand the significance of what I was viewing. As we stood on the top of the Acropolis, near the Parthenon, our guide pointed out all the traffic below. With tears in his eyes, he remarked, "This is what is destroying us." He was referring to the decaying of the marble statues and structures caused by carbon dioxide from the cars.

Our group had decided to go to a Taverna (a small Greek restaurant). But as a surprise, Jim had asked the concierge for the name of a restaurant where he could take his best girl. The one he recommended was in downtown Athens, small and delightful. As we entered, the smell of lamb, garlic, and warm bread filled my nostrils. The food tasted even better than its aroma.

As we left, the maitre'd invited us to sign the guest register. I was amazed at how many celebrity names I recognized. The taxi driver from the hotel then drove us to the 'Taverna,' where our fellow travelers were enjoying a Greek band, lots of beer, and dancing. I wondered why the customers placed pottery plates on the stage and promptly stomped on them until broken. I learned it was a Greek tradition to ward off evil spirits.

Jim spied another man smoking a cigar, and we joined him. He and his wife were from Ireland and had been to Saudi Arabia to make a lot of money. Now they were on their way home to open an Irish pub.

The next day our bus tour took us over the high bridge across the Corinth Canal, a sea-level canal that connects the Aegean and Adriatic Seas. At an outdoor amphitheater, carved out of a hillside thousands of years ago, our guide left us near the top row of seats and went down to the stage. Although he spoke in a normal voice, we could understand every word. *What secrets about acoustics did the Ancient Greeks have?*

Piraeus, the port for Athens, is on the Aegean Sea. There, our Greek ship, Europa, was waiting to take us to ports in Turkey, Ephesus, Patmos, and Rhodes.

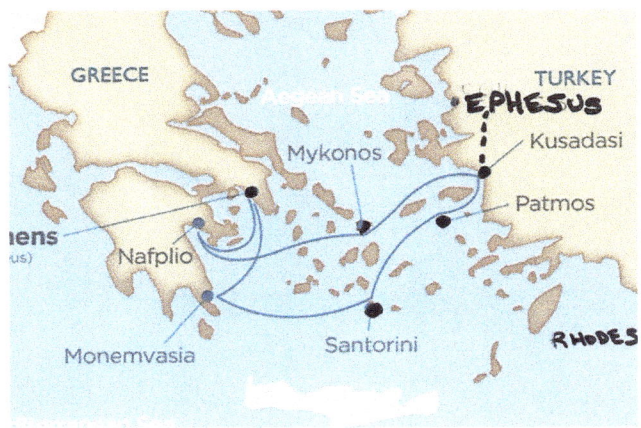

Map of the Greek Islands

Christian tradition believes when Saint John was persecuted for his faith, he was exiled to Patmos, where it is also believed John wrote the Book of Revelation. An uphill walk took us to the cave where a shrine was dedicated to John.

There were vineyards all around. From the top of a small mountain my eye caught a path that led down towards the harbor where we could see our ship at the dock. Near the path was a small house. As we descended on the path, an elderly lady beckoned us to join her on the porch, which had an "awning" made of grape vines.

She offered us a very small cup of very strong coffee. I had noticed that she wore a small Canadian-flag pin. She asked if we were Canadian. Wishing I had an American- flag pin to give her, I said, "No, we are Americans."

She escorted us back to the path, cut some beautiful roses and gave them to me. I hoped no one would think I had cut the roses myself. Back in our ship's cabin, I found a container so I could put them in water. They lasted all the way to the Island of Rhodes.

CHAPTER 12
A UNIQUE YACHT CRUISE

My favorite Tour Company, Tauck Tours, was offering a one-time trip on a private Greek yacht. The company is owned and operated by the Tauck family and is based in Wilton, Connecticut. It was 1993, I was sixty years old, and my friend Jim would again be my travel companion.

We flew to Spain, where we met our group and boarded a bus in Barcelona. We traveled through coastal France, stopped at Cannes to see where the film festival was held, and ended up in Monaco, on the French Riviera.

A tiny, beautiful, and very rich country

Boarding the yacht that was anchored in Port Hercules, we settled into our stateroom. It contained a large bedroom-sitting area and a private bathroom with a tub and shower. On the outside wall were two large picture windows beneath which were two twin beds.

The head of each bed could be elevated, which was nice for observing the water rushing around the bow, but also for reading. Our first night, after a light supper, we walked uphill to the Monte Carlo casino. I'm not a gambler, so I put a few coins in the one-armed bandits (slot machines with a handle). To my surprise, I won enough money to fill a souvenir plastic container.

Pictures cannot even begin to show the beauty of this tiny country. Of course, we saw Grace Kelly and Prince Rainier's lovely home, (Palace) and the curving road used for the motor car race, the F1, Monaco Grand Prix. It is noted that drivers may need to upshift gears 25 times during the hilly race, and the same number is true for downshifts. It was on this road that Princess Grace was fatally injured at age 52 when she suffered a stroke while driving home from Monaco with her seventeen-year-old daughter, Stephanie. Incapacitated from the medical event, she lost control of the car and drove off the precipitous mountain, dropping 100 feet down a ravine.

The following morning our yacht, carrying about 36 people,

mostly crew, left port and sailed south toward the French coastline. Mediterranean food was new to me. I had heard of the pastry, Baklava, walnuts and honey, but Pastitsio, much like Italian lasagna topped with bechamel sauce instead of mozzarella cheese) was my favorite. I also discovered the liquor Ouzo released many inhibitions, like dancing with the ship's captain, or hearing "Opa!" which means to jump and is generally meant as a compliment.

Arriving at the first French port, we exited the ship via a diving platform at the stern or rear of the yacht. It was so beautiful, but so were all the ports along the way. After a day of touring, we headed for Naples. Jim remarked this was a much nicer way to visit Italy, instead of fighting your way up the entire peninsula as he had done in World War II.

Disembarking at Capri, I looked forward to the rowboat ride to visit the Blue Grotto, one of the 7 natural wonders of the world. My mom had told me that you must enter the cave by boat. But there is a low clearance, and she had to duck down to avoid hitting her head. The bright blue water was so beautiful and an almost unbelievable color. I had visited Capri twice before, but never succeeded in experiencing this amazing place. And I wouldn't get to see it on this trip either. A passenger on the yacht developed appendicitis and had to be flown to Naples.

One evening as we continued sailing south, we saw the island of Stromboli off the starboard side. A very large glow lit up the sky and we could see fire in the night sky. Mount Stromboli is one of three active volcanoes in Italy; the other two are Etna and Vesuvius; but Stromboli has exhibited nearly constant lava flow for over 2000 years. I was privileged to visit all three.

Stromboli

That night we had heavy, rolling seas. Spotlights placed on the bow of the ship illuminated the frothy waves as we sailed the Tyrrhenian Sea. The next morning, at breakfast, one older guest commented that he had sat up all night during the storm wearing his life jacket. He said he spent the time reviewing his life and decided he was ready to die. It made me think about my own life. *What is ahead? Was I ready to die?* Thoughts of my past mistakes, wrong choices, having hurt friends with nasty comments all seeped into my memory.

I recalled one particularly painful experience when our family had first arrived in New York. I was in the eighth grade, and my Girl Scout troop visited the Statue of Liberty. It was crowded, and we had to wait a long time on the circular steps leading to the Crown. I don't know why, but I took out a pencil and wrote my name, address, and phone number on the newly-painted beige wall of the stairwell.

The following week, after Dad came home from work and we had finished dinner, he showed me a letter he had received from the National Park Service, who are charged with the care of the Statue of Liberty. They requested he contact them.

The Telephone Company was on strike, so Dad had to take the

ferry over to Liberty Island. They showed Dad my graffiti. I then learned that the fine for defacing a National Monument was $500.

Dad said, "Of course this would change our vacation plans in order to pay the fine."

My mom added, "Fools' names, like monkey faces, always appear in public places."

I was so upset, trying to figure out how I could undo what I had done. The fact that I was in a Girl Scout uniform made it even worse. I was not a city girl, and I was not at all sophisticated. My mother could see my angst and she implored my father, "Tell her, she has suffered enough."

After a day or so, Dad finally told me that because my graffiti had been drawn in pencil, not lipstick, the fine would be waived, and punishment was left up to him.

I remembered a song Frank Sinatra sang in 1969, "My Way." Some of the lyrics were: "Regrets, I have a few," it began. "...I bit off more than I could chew.... But I did it my way!" was stuck in my brain.

CHAPTER 13
HAPPY BIRTHDAY TO ME

In 1998, I celebrated a milestone. That is the year I turned sixty-five, and I wasn't sure how I would mark the occasion. One evening, I was at home looking through a magazine when I came upon an article about an old sailing boat, the Stephen Taber.

Stephen Taber

The ship was built in 1871 and is the oldest documented sailing vessel in the United States. Originally, it was used to transport Vermont granite to Brooklyn to be used in constructing the Brooklyn Bridge. With an over-all length of 110 feet, it is a centerboard schooner, designed to navigate in shallow waters. The ship would take guests on short sails, leaving from Rockland, Maine. Only twenty-two passengers are permitted.

I had always enjoyed being on the water, so I decided to call for information. I spoke with the captain's wife, who was also head cook and bottle washer, as well as an important member of the crew. She encouraged me to sail with them and suggested that as a single passenger I should take one of the bunks in the galley (kitchen) area.

In August 1998, I flew from Long Island's MacArthur Airport to Boston, Massachusetts, where I boarded a bus to the town of Rockland. I boarded the two-masted ship in the afternoon. Despite its age, it looked seaworthy. Following the captain's advice, I walked back into town to the local hardware store, where I purchased some foul-weather gear. If it was not used, I could return it.

Once back at the schooner, I was shown my space toward the bow (front) on the port (left) side of the ship—very close quarters. I could not even sit up straight. The "necessities" for me and the crew was a head (toilet) located in a cabinet on the deck.

A lovely flower arrangement greeted me on the bunk bed. The card read, "Dear Mom, Happy birthday. Have fun. Love, Your Kids." It was my 65th Birthday, and I would celebrate it on my own, sailing the waters of Maine. Sadly, the captain's wife was ill, so a man whose name I don't remember would be taking her place in the kitchen for the journey. Upon meeting me, he commented on the flowers that had been sent to me. I told him they were from my children, who were a little concerned about my sailing on such an old ship. Early in the trip, I asked the cook's helper if I could use some water in the galley.

"No," he replied. "The cook does not want any guest to be in his work area."

A little later, the helper returned with a message from the cook. He said, "If she is sharing our kitchen, she can most certainly use the water."

The food on board was delicious, served buffet-style on deck. There were tempting soups, fresh salads, great bread, and even a lobster cookout on the beach. Desserts were outstanding.

One evening the cook appeared, carrying a lemon-poppy cake, topped with birthday candles. Everyone sang 'happy birthday' to me. I asked the cook how he knew it was my birthday.

Shyly, he admitted he had read the card on the flower arrangement. I shared my story with the others, telling them about my good friend and travel companion, Jim, and how he was prone to seasickness and did not like to sail, so when I had told him about the schooner, he encouraged me to go solo. His friends suggested that I had selected a "singles cruise," looking to meet someone else.

Hearing this, the captain suggested that we take a picture of me surrounded by all the male passengers. I could then explain to Jim that it was only after I arrived at the dock that I learned that there would be only male guests on our journey.

Each evening near sundown, we dropped anchor and, with Captain Barnes playing the bagpipes or his guitar (he alternated them), the colors were lowered.

One evening, we stopped in a small cove, and as the flag was being lowered, one of the crew members shot off the small cannon. You could hear echoes of the boom reverberate around the cove. That night, I also heard my first loon call, a long mournful cry. Loons are large diving birds that have red eyes to allow for sight under the water.

Some of my fellow passengers were serious sailors and challenged Captain Barnes to show them how the Stephen Taber could really perform. Happy to oblige, the captain headed to the open waters of Penobscot Bay.

With the sails now full of wind, we were really sailing. It was exhilarating! Soon, the captain noticed a sleek, white sailing schooner, much larger than ours, closing in behind us. He muttered, "I can't believe they are going to woosh us (take our wind)."

Yes, they whooshed us good. As they passed close to windward, the uniformed crew, lined up along the rail, waved and shouted "Hip, hip, hooray!" They easily pulled ahead.

On its stern, we could see the name "Canadian Merchant Marine Training Vessel."

Too soon our sailing trip was over. I had been fortunate, the weather was perfect and I didn't have to use the yellow foul weather gear. Upon departing the ship, I walked back into the town of Rockland to return my unused foul-weather gear. During the walk, I noticed the Farnsworth Art Museum where Andrew Wyeth, who had a home in nearby Cushing, had some of his paintings on display. I stopped in for a quick visit.

After a pleasant dinner on my own, and an overnight at a local inn, I returned home to beautiful Long Island. To the surprise of many, traveling had become my passion. And this would not be my last solo adventure.

CHAPTER 14
MANY BLESSINGS

Although I was living life on my own, I have been blessed with seven grandchildren, followed eventually by eight great-grandchildren (soon to be nine). I believe each person who comes into your life adds another dimension to it. Everyone has their own stories to tell and their own memories to provide. For each of my grandchildren, I will present a sample of the many precious memories they have given me.

SUE'S GRANDCHILREN

Sue's grandchildren (l to r) Sarah Reisert, Jessica Castoro, Lawrence McClure, Matt Reisert, Nicky Greco, Tyler Kuchenbrod, Jenifer Kuchenbrod, in 2021

My granddaughter Sarah, daughter of Cheryl and Chris, graduated from Villanova and obtained her master's degree from Drexel University. She lives and works near Philadelphia. She always loved to read, so when her birthday list, when she was a freshman at Our Lady of Mercy Academy in Syosset, included a book title, I wasn't surprised.

First, I read a review of the book she named, then I read the book. Wow! Child abuse, incest, a dysfunctional family and painful experiences were but a few of the written episodes described on the back of the book she had chosen. Concerned, I asked my daughter if she realized what her teenage daughter was reading. Learning of my concern, Sarah called me and said, "Don't worry, Grandma, it's just an adult fairy tale!"

Sarah's brother, Matt, told me about his college investment course that mentioned the advantages of owning stock and receiving dividend checks, reminding me that one year I had given each of the grandchildren a single share of a stock. He told me that one day, the professor asked if any of the students owned stock and had ever received a dividend check. Matt raised his hand. "How much was the dividend?" the professor asked him. Matt replied, "Fifty cents!"

Matt has remained on Long Island and with his wife Megan, has provided me with two great-grandchildren, Ava and Ella.

Linda and Sam's son, Lawrence, who lives in Florida, asked me during one of our phone conversations to play golf with him . *Where can you find fresh air, mild exercise, and nice people? On the golf course, I thought.*

On my next visit, I soon discovered that what he really wanted to do was drive the golf cart. He was too young for a driver's license. Eventually, he became both a good driver and a good golfer. He now serves as a Representative in the Florida State Legislature. He and his wife Courtney have a daughter, Savannah, and are soon expecting another one, who will be called Madeline.

My grandson, Nicholas, Lori and Nick's son, married Jennifer Burns in 2010, and they have provided me with two great-grandchildren, Nicolas and Brianna.

Nicholas, whom we all call "Nicky," came to Long Island to live with me while finishing his last year of college and then started commuting to his first job in New York City.

Early one morning, I was reading an article in *The New York Times* about a spray-on condom. The idea had been inspired by the mechanics of a drive-through car wash. Finding it interesting, I read the article to Nicky. He beat a hasty retreat to his car and then called his cousin, Matt, breathlessly asking, "Do you know what Grandma hit me with the first thing this morning?"

Nicky's sister, Jessica, married Jon Castoro in 2017, and they have produced two more great-grandchildren, Emelia and a little boy, Nathan ("Nate" for short) who was born in February, 2023, weighing in at 12 pounds! He is great-grandchild number 7.

Jessica, who "inherited" my love of dance, went to St. John's

University where she received her BS and master's degrees in speech therapy. She originally enrolled in the university's Performing Arts Program that provided multiple opportunities.

One time, I accompanied her parents and several friends to see her dance in the "kit kat" chorus of *Cabaret*. Like the other dancers, she appeared in a skimpy costume and performed limbering up movements of stretching, splits and other moves designed to "establish" an atmosphere of" jaded decadence."

At one point, my other "son" Steve, Jessica's godfather, leaned over and said to me, "This is upsetting to see Jessica do these sexy movements."

"She is only dancing," I replied.

He rolled his eyes. "Does she have to be so good at it?"

My son, Charlie married Ursula Spitzer in September, 1987. Their son Tyler was born in November, 1992 and his sister, Jennifer Rae joined the family in October 1995.

Tyler married Taylor Tireili in 2019 and they have a son, Samuel, another great-grandchild.

Tyler had attended Lutheran High School in Oyster Bay. One afternoon, I went to pick him up and waited in the car for him. At 3 pm, the school's doors opened, and a flood of students burst out. Tyler jumped into the backseat of the car and off we went toward home in Kings Park.

As we drove, he told me the story he had just heard in Chapel: It was Christmas and two children, a boy and a girl, accepted a beautifully wrapped present from a wealthy aunt. In past years she had always given them $50, so the boy opened the box, hoping to find the $50 bill. Instead, he found a pair of gloves. In disgust, he threw the whole package into the fire. His sister then opened her gift. She had also received gloves. Sliding her hand into the glove, her fingers found a crisp $50 bill. No further words needed from me.

Charlie and Ursula's daughter, Jennifer, is a teacher. When she was about twelve years old, she was walking with me on one of Long Island's north shore beaches when we found the shell from a horseshoe crab. Strange, but I had just been reading about this "important diminutive armor-plated tank that had survived for at least 450 million years."

I told Jessica that their millions of eggs feed many types of marine life. But they have been over-harvested for bait and for their blue blood. For instance, this blood is used for a standard test, limulus amoebocytes, whose unique attribute is testing for cleanliness of medical devices. "If a foreign body gets into a horseshoe crab's blood, it is immediately attacked by the immune system and clots around the infection."

Further adding to Jennifer's knowledge, I mentioned that horseshoe crabs mate on the first full moon in May. The following May, at the full moon, Jennifer informed her startled mom that the horseshoe crabs would be mating that night. All together, these children and grandchildren, and their spouses, plus the great-grandchildren, make up my family, for which I am extremely grateful, and of which I am very proud.

CHAPTER 15
CHINA FOR ONE

I wanted to see China. It seemed a strange, mysterious place. Several of my traveling companions said they would like to go with me, but time, money, and other things interfered. I decided to try a Tauck Tour as a single person. My granddaughter Jessica was living at my house while finishing grad school, so she would be able to look after things while I was away.

That November, I boarded a 747 plane of China Airlines, one of the state-owned national carriers of the Republic of China and flew northwest on the great-circle route from JFK Airport non-stop to Hong Kong. The flight was over 6800 miles in 14 hours, depending on the prevailing winds.

The airline food was excellent; very competent flight attendants made sure we were comfortable. The passengers were a mixture of Asian and other nationalities. Knowing how important it is to exercise while flying long distances, from time to time I would walk up one aisle and down the other.

During one of those walks I paused for a moment in the galley area and looked out one of the small windows, staring into the darkness. Feeling a gentle tap on my shoulder, I turned to see a short, older, Asian man, whose friendly smile revealed a few missing teeth.

He asked, "You Amelican?" His accent was thick, but I understood his question.

I nodded in the affirmative, surprised when he began singing "God Bless Amelica."

I joined in as did some of the other passengers. Surely, this was going to be a special trip.

My room on the 98th floor of the Ritz Carlton Hotel was beyond amazing, providing a panoramic view of Hong Kong harbor. A bowl of fresh fruit welcomed me. The bathroom had two separate chambers. One held the toilet with a heated seat. The other had a bidet. TV programs were viewable in the bathroom mirror. The large white bathtub with side jets looked appealing, particularly after such a long flight.

Most astonishing to me was a message from my son Charles: "If possible, Mom, could you call me?"

I rushed to the hotel's business office where they helped me place the call. Our oil-fired burner wouldn't work. It was November and cold in Long Island, which meant my granddaughter, Jessica, had no heat. I asked Charles to get it repaired. He reported that it was beyond repair, so I told him to get a new one.

I later learned that Jessica had called my service company. They came and said it was fixed, but it still didn't work. She called again, and a different service man came and said it was a good thing it didn't work because it was emitting carbon monoxide. Thankfully, everyone was okay.

Jessica later remarked to me, "I could have died."

I spent some time visiting the street markets in Kowloon, riding the Star ferry, and sampling different foods. A fellow passenger on the tour mentioned to me that she had a bad back and that flying had exacerbated the problem. She wondered about getting a massage at the hotel. I was delighted to learn there was another single woman on the tour and told her I would join her. We called the concierge to book the appointment, but we were told they were completely booked.

Overhearing our problem, our young, attractive, female Chinese guide offered to take us to her massage parlor, which was within walking distance from the hotel. Another guide, male, asked to join us. The massage room was full of tables separated by curtains.

We could hear our male guide giggling as he reacted to the massage and accompanying foot bath. My new friend confided she was glad we were together for such an adventure.

I cannot recall the actual order in which we visited the many sights in China, but we took a short flight to Xian to see the famous terra-cotta soldiers. The collection, which was discovered relatively recently, included more than 8,000 life-sized soldiers in a military array. They had been buried with Emperor Qin in 210 BCE. The faces of the soldiers varied.

There also were horses, chariots, and many other artifacts that the emperor felt he would need in the afterlife. His burial site covered many acres. Experts predict that when completely uncovered the number of soldiers will approach 16,000.

I wonder what I might take with me in the afterlife. Personally, I feel it is more important to live life now, to follow the Golden Rule, and hopefully leave something behind that will contribute to peace among people.

The Great Wall in China

We walked on the Great Wall, watched two baby pandas enjoy their breakfast of bamboo shoots, and marveled at the massive, three-gorges dam in the Yangtze River. Stunned at the magnitude of the dam, I began to daydream. When I heard someone from our group call out "Susanah! Come on!" I was so grateful. Otherwise, I might still be lost somewhere in China.

As a side trip, we visited a dispossessed farmer whose former land was now under water. His new home was small and had an earthen floor. Tools were neatly arranged on the walls. Shoes were arrayed on the ground, outside the entrance door. Chickens and a rooster scratched for seeds near the garden.

The old farmer explained, through an interpreter, that the government had given him new land away from the flooded area, plus a condominium. But he wanted to farm and have his own home.

So, he gave the condo to his son and built this typical small wooden house for himself.

For a thrill, we rode one of China's new bullet trains from Beijing to a nearby city. Whizzing through the countryside at 150 mph was intoxicating.

After boarding a ship for a three-day cruise up the Yangtze River, we had lunch while we enjoyed a dance presentation by lovely Chinese women. "Yangtze" is a Chinese word for "Long River." It extends nearly 900 miles from Tibet to Shanghai. It is a working river. We saw much commerce and other activity while traveling upstream.

Sailing up the Yangtze River in China

My cabin had a small outside balcony where I could sit and study the steep walls of the gorge. A butterfly landed on the railing and stayed a while, enjoying the warm sun with me.

Each morning, just after sunrise, an aging Chinese woman gave lessons in Tai Chi on the upper bow deck. Tai Chi is a form of internal martial arts known for defense, health benefits, and meditation. Our excellent teacher was patient and encouraged me to keep practicing.

We left the ship to board a sampan (small wooden boat). The single oarsman propelled us into a small gorge. At first the sampan looked unstable and rickety, but it turned out to provide a "hallmark moment" of beautiful scenery, many caves, wildflowers, and trees seemingly growing out of the rock. As we glided past a break in the side wall, we caught a glimpse of a sheep herder tending his flock.

Beijing was our last city. It has seven UNESCO heritage sites. Standing in Tiananmen Square, trying to conjure up the scene of the 1989 student-led protests for free speech and free press, I noticed some Tibetan Buddhist monks robed in ochre (Burgundy-red) robes, wearing <u>white Nike sneakers.</u> Nearby was the Forbidden City.

Beijing hosted the 2008 Summer Olympics when Michael Phelps won his seventh gold medal in the butterfly event. They continue to use the Olympic facilities for public purposes, including a very large swimming pool, basketball courts, a running track, and a soccer field.

The night before we left on our flight home, some of us realized that during our two-week tour we had purchased so much "stuff" that our suitcases couldn't handle it. We decided to venture into a street market near the hotel to buy an additional bag at a reasonable price, a farewell gesture to a fascinating country.

We walked into a non-touristy area, entered an office-type building and rode the elevator to the third floor. There I found a fake Louis Vuitton small suitcase with wheels, and was able to negotiate a good price, about half of what was initially asked. As a tourist I found my experiences on this trip were positive. There is so much to learn about China, with its long history of ancient art and culture.

CHAPTER 16
AFRICA

"Let's go to Africa," my friend and co-worker Harriet said. She dearly wanted to see the dark continent.

I replied immediately, "Yes! But only if we can go on safari with an established and well-organized tour."

It was September of 2002, and at sixty-nine, this would be my second Tauck Tour. Only this time, I would be traveling with a companion.

We flew from New York to Amsterdam, where we spent two days exploring this amazing city. From Amsterdam, the flight to Nairobi, the capital of Kenya, took over eight hours. In Nairobi we spent two days getting acquainted with the African flora and fauna. We also visited the home of Karen Bixen, the author of the book *Out of Africa*. She had spent 17 years in Africa helping the native people. She taught them about medicine, reading, and writing skills.

In the style of upper-class Britons, she also taught them to serve meals always wearing white jackets and white gloves. The movie *Out of Africa* starring Robert Redford and Meryl Streep, was loosely based on her book. Neither the book nor the movie could have prepared us for the extraordinary experiences we were about to enjoy.

A short flight in a small plane carried our party of six and the guide from Nairobi to the "lodge," nestled in the shoulder of the Serengeti. The lodge was surrounded by high fences and an electric gate. The Serengeti, an open area of 12,000 square miles, is one of the ten wonders of the natural world. The name is from the Maasai language and means "endless plains."

At the lodge, four of us then hopped aboard a canopied jeep, which took us to a variety of places. As we drove along, we saw all of the "big five" animals that were originally known to be the dangerous and most difficult to hunt—lions, leopards, rhinos, elephants, and African buffalo.

Sue and overweight friend at lunch in Kenya

We also saw many other exotic animals roaming free – wildebeests trying to cross a large stream and crocodiles laying in the stream, their eyes just showing above the water, waiting to capture a small or injured animal.

The next morning, as dawn was breaking, we drove to a huge clearing where a hot-air balloon was being inflated. It was decorated with bright colors of red, orange, and brown and had big black letters spelling out "Tauck Tours."

After we climbed aboard a large basket that hung below the

colorful balloon, we lifted into the air — silently. The only noise was the air heater, whose spurts of hot air kept us on track. Slowly we floated above the Serengeti Plain and watched the bi-annual migrations of the Wildebeest and other animals. As we neared the border with Tanzania, we softly landed.

Thanks to Tauck, the six of us enjoyed a full breakfast of Eggs Benedict, chilled orange juice, a croissant, and coffee, all set on white tablecloths and served by waiters in white jackets and gloves. After breakfast, relaxed in comfortable chairs, we enjoyed our chilled Mimosa and Bloody Mary drinks and were inspired by the awesome view of Tanzania and Mount Kilimanjaro.

That evening we were loaded back into our Jeep. The dark sky was filled with millions of stars. As we moved into the jungle, our guide informed us that dinner would be served outside our compound, around a campfire. *What about all those wild animals?*

Suddenly, as we drove around a large rock, we could see a fire. Nearby was a dinner table set with fine China, a white tablecloth, crystal, and silver in a proper array. White-gloved servers offered an array of drinks.

After dinner, as we sat around the fire and chatted, we suddenly heard loud shouts, whoops, and a rustle in the bush. Out came four very tall Maasai warriors, dressed in brilliant red. They carried spears and shields but did not threaten us. Our guide said there was nothing to fear, and he explained a little of their culture.

I found it interesting that Maasai women were considered beautiful if they had shapely skulls. The warriors then danced for us, ending up with a warrior beside each woman's chair.

The guide said they would like to dance with us. He hinted that the higher you could jump, the more attractive you were. The music started and, feeling quite happy after the drinks, I jumped as high as I could.

When we returned to our chairs, we were told that we had danced the Maasai's Matrimonial Dance. I looked way up to the face of my dancing partner. In a deep, resonant voice he announced, "You is my woman now."

Married again?

"You is my woman now!"

The last story from Africa I would like to share with you is, for me, the best one. Local people who worked at our lodge arranged for us to visit their village. On the way there, we were told not to look down upon their way of life.

Their low-to-the-ground huts had small entrances. But once inside, they were quite comfortable. The day was warm. Outside, cows and donkeys stayed in the shade, rabbits and chickens scratched the ground. Small children gave each of us a present, a bracelet they had made from cow bone, marked in brown stripes.

As we walked up a small incline, there was a shelter from the sun, called a lanai, built from tree branches that provided amazingly good shade. Standing beneath it were three very tall Maasai warrior chiefs. They greeted us in English and thanked us for coming to their beautiful country. They told us that some village people worked at the lodge and had seen the television reports of the terrorist attack on the World Trade Center in New York City.

One of the chiefs then said, "We have everything we need, enough to eat, shelter, and family, but most of all we have no enemies." He continued, "We felt so sad when we heard about all the pain and suffering in America. We continue to send our prayers and love to all Americans."

Waiting to board the jumbo jet at Nairobi's Jomo Kenyatta International airport, I thought about how fortunate I was to have experienced a trip like this! Later, looking at the globe, I see that our world is indeed large, but it is also very small.

CHAPTER 17
SOUTH AMERICA

Over the next several years, I would make two trips to South America, and I would visit Iceland. In Brazil, I got to attend Mardi Gras, an old French tradition with an interesting history. I had loved watching on TV the parade and costumes in the New Orleans celebration. But I never thought I would actually see the celebration (Entrudo) in Rio De Janeiro.

Jim suggested we go, so I asked the gal from the travel agency who had planned my family trip to Hawaii to make the arrangements for Brazil. We took a chartered, direct flight from New York to Rio.

While on the plane, the pilot made an announcement. "If the passengers seated on the right side of the aircraft look out their window, they will see a large green stripe painted on the ground. That is the equator," he said.

Some of the passengers seated on the left side of the plane, got up and rushed to a window on the right side to see this special "sight." Of course, the pilot was simply being playful.

Unfortunately, I had not communicated to the travel agent our ideas for the trip. So, she planned a relaxing vacation at a resort on the outskirts of Rio, on the beach. She did not give us any ideas for visits to places that we, as first-time visitors, might be interested in. We had to find our own amusements.

The waves at the beach looked fierce, but Jim had been a lifeguard and wanted to have a swim. Although it was early in the morning, the sand was so hot the heat burned through our beach slippers. We were warned about the adorable children who were well-skilled in stealing and we were strongly cautioned, "Do not take anything to the beach, just the hotel towel."

There were vendors on the beach selling clothes, linens, trinkets, jewelry, embroidered tablecloths and napkins. I admired a set of eight napkins and a tablecloth with beautiful lacework, crocheted with cutout designs. I told the vendor I had left my money in the hotel. When we left the beach the vendor followed us to the hotel, which was well guarded by hotel security. Showing concern for my safety, one of the guards went with me to get the money to purchase the set, and then he paid the vendor.

H. Stern, a well-known jewelry chain, offered us a ride in a limousine from the resort to downtown Rio to visit their workplace and retail store. Jim, being in the jewelry business, always traveled with his "loupe" (a small magnifying glass used to inspect stones for the three C's—clarity, color, and cracks).

While the show room was impressive, and watching the gem setters was most interesting, the prices at H. Stern were very expensive. When we showed no interest in purchasing anything, we were politely "shown the door." *Can you imagine? There was no offer of a return limo ride to our resort.*

Portuguese is the most often spoken language in Rio, although Spanish and Italian are readily understood, as is English in some places. We were able to find a place for lunch. I ordered hard boiled eggs and was surprised that the small shell (think pigeon) was blue. Later, we went to Copacabana and sat at an outdoor restaurant, located on Portuguese Beach walkway. The gray and white tiled wave pattern on the boardwalk was the perfect setting for watching the shapely Bikini-clad girls.

The cog train up to the large statue of Christ the Redeemer and base at the top of Corcovado was a wonderful way to see the entire area of Rio de Janeiro.

Christ the Redeemer statue overlooking Rio de Janeiro

We sadly left Rio's tropical climate to return to cold New York. It was a long flight, and I was startled when the captain told us a very severe winter storm had developed and that most of the Northeast airports were closed. We would have to land early and were asked to vote if we wanted to land in Orlando, Florida, or Atlanta, Georgia.

I didn't participate in the vote, because I figured this was just another of the pilot's "green stripe on the ground" jokes. So, I took a nap. The vote was for Orlando, as the newly opened Walt Disney World resort was there.

The next thing I heard was an announcement that said that we were approaching the Orlando airport. When we landed, the pilot apologized for the delay, explaining that they had been battling 250 mph headwinds.

The second day of the trip we were finally on our way home. This plane needed to get back to New York as they were committed to another charter flight. But the New York airports were still closed. We landed in Philadelphia and exited down a ramp onto a runway covered with two feet of snow. Using the blankets from the plane for cover over our tropical clothing, we were shown to school buses for the chilly ride to Manhattan.

Nothing was moving in New York City. Scrambling for a room at the Hotel Pennsylvania, we were lucky to secure a small room next to the bank of noisy elevators. The Long Island railroad had some trains running, but we had to change in Jamaica. The sign indicated our train was on Platform B. I had packed way too much stuff and had a large, heavy suitcase.

Just as we had climbed up to Platform B, we were informed of a change of platforms. I had to lug this big, heavy, red suitcase down a flight of stairs and then climb up other stairs to the correct platform. *This was before some genius thought of wheels for suitcases.*

On this trip I learned two things for the future. I would plan my visits more carefully, and I would certainly pack much less stuff.

My next trip to South America was with Harriet to Buenos Aires, the capital city of Argentina, known as "the city that never sleeps." One day in 2009 Harriet, the Administrative Assistant at the Library, asked me at a meeting of our book club if I would be interested in a short visit to Argentina. Needless to say, I jumped at the thought. She said one of her best friends who was a travel agent would plan the trip for us.

We arrived at about 4 pm. Our hotel was luxurious and delightful. After a brief rest, we went down to the lobby and asked the concierge to recommend a good restaurant for dinner. He said the best steak house in town was just down the block from the hotel and that Argentina is known globally for its excellent beef. *He was correct about the food.*

Both of us had already seen the play *Evita*, but Harriet wanted to see it again with a Spanish dialogue, so we headed for the theater district. Although I could not understand a word, watching the show in Spanish produced a much stronger emotional reaction than did the Broadway version.

After the show, we looked for and found the small bar noted for being one of the sites where the Tango dance originated. Inside, the stage was small and the music loud. We sat on high stools at a table just big enough to hold our two wine glasses. The male dancer was dressed in a tight black outfit with pointed black shoes and greased hair. His female partner wore a ruffled dress that dipped in the back and was open in the front, which showed off her amazing legs. They danced close together across the stage, strong moves punctuated with dips to the floor, hinting of an abusive relationship.

The next day we took a ferry that runs often across the Rio de la Plata from Buenos Aires to Uruguay. There, we visited a UNESCO site, enjoyed a delightful lunch in a garden restaurant, and then hired a taxi for some sight-seeing in the surrounding area before returning to our hotel on the ferry.

On our last day in Argentina, the concierge arranged for a private driver to take us to the airport. But first he was to provide us a tour around Buenos Aires, showing us various historic sites. The driver asked where we were from. When we said Long Island, he smiled and confessed he had attended C.W. Post college in Brookville.

Again, *I'm often reminded it is a small world, after all!*

Picking up on our visit to *Evita*, the driver expanded on the story of how Evita had served as a very popular First Lady while her husband, Juan Peron, was President of the country. Sadly, she died from cancer. He drove us past her grave, which was in a crypt in La Recoleta cemetery.

Our flight back to JFK was uneventful until we arrived. The airline lost Harriet's checked bag. *That was the only time in all my travels that there had been any problem with luggage.*

CHAPTER 18

A TRULY SPECIAL TRAVELING COMPANION

Retirement from the local public library, where I was now Supervisor of the Circulation Department, came in 2003 at age seventy, and I signed up for Social Security benefits.

My four children were married and had families of their own. My once too-small house was now too big. It had four bedrooms, two bathrooms, a large kitchen/family room and a finished basement, plus a driveway that could accommodate six cars. Jim and I had been good friends for many years but we had slowly drifted apart.

One afternoon, **THE PHONE RANG**. It was my eldest granddaughter, Sarah.

"I need a ride to Philadelphia for a job interview," she told me.

"Of course," I replied. I was always up for an adventure.

Sarah had applied for a position at Constitution Hall. She did the interview and got the job. Even better, we had time to visit some of the historic sites, the Philadelphia Mint, Independence Hall, the Liberty Bell, Betsy Ross house, even a ghost walk visiting possible haunted places. Little did we know she would always live in or near Philadelphia.

Our next adventure was in 2007.

THE PHONE RANG once again. This time Sarah was calling about a Carnival Cruise to Belize and other ports of call. Her traveling partner could not make the trip. She was sure my passport was in order, and as an added incentive, she said, "The ship leaves from the Port of Tampa, so you can see your daughter, Linda."

"Yes," I replied and started packing.

What she failed to tell me was that this was a singles cruise. So, there would be lots of available men looking for partners. Sarah was in her twenties, and she and her girlfriend had planned a trip intended for people their age. *(Surely, there wouldn't be any men on board looking for me.)*

Nevertheless, Sarah and I had many fun adventures. One evening while on board the ship, we wandered into the gambling area. We each had a bucket of quarters and fed the one-armed bandits (slot machines that eat quarters!). There was another area with singing and dancing.

But my favorite part of the trip was a horseback ride through a rainforest. The two of us, accompanied by a guide, rode through the palmettos and never saw another house. As we headed into a wooded area, it seemed we disturbed a million blue butterflies, who took flight all together. An amazing sight!

When regaling friends about our adventurer holiday, Sarah's friends commented to her, "I can't believe you took your grandmother on a singles cruise."

Soon, Sarah later found a job that better fitted her capabilities with a non-profit foundation. Among her responsibilities was setting up awards ceremonies. In 2009, one of the events was in Atlanta, Georgia, and Sarah invited me to join her there.

I was touched, and of course, I happily accepted.

As usual, Sarah was able to organize her work schedule, making time for us to enjoy some of the nearby historic areas. We visited Martin Luther King's home in "Sweet Auburn," the center of Black Atlanta, which is now a museum. A short train ride took us to Bulloch Hall, the home of Theodore Roosevelt's mother-in-law near

Roswell, Georgia. The docent was happy to learn that I was from Oyster Bay, New York, where Teddy had his summer retreat, Sagamore Hill.

We also toured the Roswell Mill Ruins in Old Mill Park. The mill once produced rope, tent cloth and a fine, gray-colored cloth. This cloth saved the mill when American Civil War general William Tecumseh Sherman, known to his troops as Major general Sherman, burned his way through Georgia. He did not destroy the mill, as he needed the cloth to make new uniforms for his Union soldiers.

Before returning to Atlanta, we enjoyed "high tea" at The Ginger Room," a local bakery shop in Roswell. Reservations were required, and extremely difficult to get. But Sarah had prearranged our visit, and everyone was wondering how she had managed to get us in. It was a delightful experience for us both.

The following day, after a much-needed night's sleep, Sarah and I ventured into "downtown" Atlanta. With great expectations, we went to a "touristy" area of the city for a bus tour. Sarah had reserved the tour of Atlanta's historic sites, including the graves of Confederate and Yankee soldiers. But when we arrived at the stated location, we were informed that there was no tour running at that time.

I turned to leave, but my organized companion opened her briefcase and produced a paper printed with the confirmed reservation number. After some tearful pleading, a special trolley took us on a private tour. *Leave it to Sarah to make things happen.*

Among Sarah's many talents, acting and singing are some of them. It could be in a local church, a college church choir or local theater. *Need I add belly dancing is something we both enjoyed?*

Our next adventure was in August 2012 to Santa Fe, New Mexico, for five nights of opera at the famous Santa Fe Opera, an open-air theater on Opera Drive. She had introduced me to opera at the Metropolitan Opera House in Philadelphia, listed on the National Register of Historic Places. Constructed in 1908, it was the ninth opera house built by Oscar Hammerstein, a German-born businessman, theater impresario and composer in New York City.

Daytime in Santa Fe found us exploring many activities, including outdoor yoga in one of the national parks. The instructor led us up a hill through the trees to a secluded spot, where we set up our yoga mats on the ground. It was a tranquil setting. I remember thinking how quiet it was as I lay on my mat looking up through the trees to the pristine blue sky.

Returning to Santa Fe, Sarah and I headed to the spa and readied ourselves for a massage. First, a quick dip in the outdoor pool, palm trees offering some shade, then the sweet, scented darkness of the massage room. Lunch was served in a beautiful garden.

The next day found us at Bandelier National Monument, 33,000 acres of mesa and canyons. The park ranger warned that if we saw even one flash of lightning, we should leave, no, run to our car. Flash flooding is serious and deadly.

We climbed up to the top of a small plateau and the view was awesome. A dad out hiking with his two sons inquired as to where our water bottles were. Learning we had none, he kindly shared his extra bottles with us.

After the hike, we drove down and enjoyed dinner together at the Sandia Peak Tramway, an aerial tramway adjacent to Albuquerque. It was a clear night, so we took the cable car 2.7 miles up to the top of the Sandia Mountains. The lights of Albuquerque seemed to float below us.

The city of Roswell was nearby so we drove out to visit the International UFO Museum and Research Center. In 1947, it was reported that an unidentified flying object had crashed and that an alien was recovered. Many people felt the U.S Government was not telling the whole truth. All five nights, we returned to Santa Fe to enjoy the operas.

There was so much to appreciate at the Santa Fe Opera house. First, it is an open-air theater that allows you to watch the amazing sunsets. We also enjoyed the backstage tour, seeing how much effort it takes to produce an opera.

Before returning home, we attended one of Santa Fe's many craft fairs. I saw a watch in a jewelry store and asked its price. Standing near me was a very tall, handsome Native American man. I asked him where he was from, and his reply made me shudder. His relatives, the Cherokees, had been on the Trail of Tears, the forced march ordered by Andrew Jackson in 1831. It continued for five years, was 1200 miles long, and ended in Oklahoma. He was still very angry. *It was truly a dark side of the early history of our country.*

CHAPTER 19
PLACES I WOULD LIKE TO SEE

At seventy-seven, I was physically fit, and I still enjoyed traveling; I was always looking for my next adventure. Near the top of my list of "Places I Would Like to See" was the Passion Play in Oberammergau, a small Bavarian village in Germany.

In the 17th century, the Thirty Years' War took place in central Europe, causing much poverty and sickness. Many people died of the plague known as the "Black Death." In 1633, Catholic residents of the village prayed to God that if they would be spared from the Black Death, every ten years they would perform a 'passion play' about the suffering, death and resurrection of Jesus Christ.

My parents had attended the Oberammergau Passion Play back in 1960, and during the ride home from the airport, they told me what a moving experience it had been. Right then, I hoped that one day I would be able to see it for myself. .But "every ten years" passed so quickly, and forty years later, I suddenly realized If I didn't go in 2010, at age seventy-seven, I might not be able to make it in 2020. So, I needed to go NOW!

However, my usual traveling companions were not interested. I wasn't going to let that stop me, so I began researching ways to visit on my own. I learned that Pilgrim Tours offered a combined trip to Oberammergau and Israel. Another of my top of the list places was the Holy Land, so I signed up to go solo.

After making the necessary arrangements, I boarded a flight at New York's JFK airport and flew many hours to Berlin. But the plane was delayed, and I almost missed my connecting flight to the Bavarian village of Oberammergau.

When we finally landed that warm afternoon, I had enough time for a cable-car ride to the top of a nearby mountain. As the guide pointed out, on a clear day we could see Munich beyond the Bavarian mountains and you could also see the Alps of Switzerland. A beautiful and amazing sight.

Once at the hotel, I met my assigned roommate, who was from Seattle. She was a bit older than I expected, and she had some health issues, but we got along fine. Foot problems limited her walking, so most of the time she sat on the bus and worked on Sudoku puzzles. She had little interest in the Oberammergau part of the trip; she really wanted to see Israel.

The Oberammergau Passion Play was, of course, impressive. Originally, it was performed in a barn. But as it became more popular, it was moved to a large stage in a huge, outdoor amphitheater filled with hundreds of people. There were animals and many characters.

Scene from the Oberammergau Passion Play in 2010

For centuries, the actors have all been residents of the tiny village, with a population of about 5,000. Probably the most impressive part was the crucifixion scene. Next stop, Israel.

Jerusalem sits between the Mediterranean and the Dead Seas. It is over 5000 years in existence and one of the oldest cities in the world. It is considered holy by each of the three major Abrahamic religions—Judaism, Christianity, and Islam.

Our first night in Jerusalem, we dined in our hotel, which was lovely, clean, and conveniently located. After the meal, our group of twelve gathered in a conference room for an overview of the trip. Our group included, in addition to my roommate and me, an older couple who were returning to their homeland, two pastors and their wives, and two Mennonite girls, who always wore ankle length dresses and some type of head covering.

Our tour guide in Israel was a young German-Jewish man whose family had fled persecution in Germany. He attended school in Israel, and as he remarked, "He became a Christian, married a Christian girl, and broke his mother's heart."

He loved Israel and its history. In most instances, when indicating the locations of various points in the biblical stories of Jesus' arrest, trial, crucifixion, and burial, he would begin by stating "we think this is where..." Of course, no one really knew. When he noticed that some in our group were gathering pamphlets, souvenirs, and other small items, he gave each of us a small nylon backpack labeled "Pilgrim Tours."

The small city of Jerusalem contains many historic sites. As a Christian, I wanted to see the places mentioned in the Bible, and I did. We visited Church of the Holy Sepulcher, Western wall, Dome of the Rock, Temple Mount, and Via Dolorosa Street, all within a two-plus mile radius.

We shared Communion in the garden at Golgotha, where it is believed Jesus was taken after his crucifixion. One of my favorite sites was a re-creation of a small, working village, similar to the Old Bethpage Village on Long Island. It contained olive trees, chickens and animals, a grape press, a well, and a small house. Local people clad in peasant dress worked at carpentry and basket weaving. We also saw farm animals grazing in the pasture, an old man using a wine press, and olive trees sheltering a group of donkeys. It all generated a feeling of moving back in time.

The village guide ended her presentation by giving each one of our group a small replica of an oil lamp. She cautioned us that when we went through customs on our return home, just say "No" when the security agent asks if anyone had given you anything.

It seems that in 1986 a plot to blow up an Israeli aircraft had been uncovered. An unsuspecting pregnant woman was given a package by her Jordanian boyfriend to carry with her on her flight from London to Israel. An alert security official at El Al Airlines in London's Heathrow Airport, through close questioning, sensed something was not quite right. He eventually uncovered a 1.5kg bomb in the package given to her by the Jordanian boyfriend. It was timed to go off mid-flight and would have killed 307 people, including the unsuspecting girl herself. As a result, Israel developed one of the strictest security systems anywhere. Ben Gurion Airport is now considered the most secure airport in the world.

Outside the old walled city, we visited the Praetorium, the Governors' compound where Pontius Pilate stayed when in Jerusalem, and we came toward the place where Jesus was sentenced and held overnight. I noticed that for his explanations our guide was using a diorama and was reading from the Bible. But I wanted to see the actual place, so I left the "lecture" and walked downhill to arrive at a large, white building where I saw the room purported to be the place where Jesus had been held.

And naturally I visited the gift shop. Suddenly I realized I would be late returning to the bus. So, I quickly paid for my gifts and ran uphill, on cobblestones, to the parking lot. The driver had wanted to leave without me, but to stop him, one of the couples got off the bus, saw me, and called out "Hurry, Susanah!"

In a boat modeled after the fishing boats of biblical times, we sailed on the Sea of Galilee. I wondered if the others, while gazing at the shore and low hills, shared my vision of Jesus with Peter, working their fishing nets in a crude boat. Then I noticed, a short distance away, a power boat towing a water skier.

Before we left the area, of course I had to try swimming in the Dead Sea. It was impossible to sink, because of the high density of salt. I think we were all wishing we could spend more time in Israel, but in the early evening our group arrived at the Ben Gurion Airport for our return to the United States. It was a large facility, well lit, and the clear, posted directions were easy to follow. At the security area, we were waiting in line to have our luggage examined. I noticed a young, attractive female, dressed in black pants, with an official-looking badge pinned to her crisp white shirt. She had a gun holstered on her belt.

She asked me to please step out of the line. After carefully inspecting my passport, she inquired, "Why, as a single woman, did you travel to Israel, by yourself?" My answer seemed weak. I wanted to visit both Germany and Israel and I could not find anyone to come with me. We chatted about my family.

Her next question was, "Has anyone given you anything to take home?"

Remembering the warning by the Village Guide about the little souvenir oil lamp, I lied. "No," I replied.

Inspectors are especially trained in observing reactions, and she pressed on. "Have you traveled the whole trip with these two Amish girls that are ahead of you in line?"

I smiled and replied, "Yes."

Her eyes narrowed. "Were you given a Pilgrim Tour blue Nylon bag like theirs?"

When I answered "yes," the Inspector replied in a hardened tone, "But you just told me no one gave you anything while you were visiting Israel."

The Israeli tote bag that Sue forgot to declare at Ben Gurion airport

WOW! I was caught, and for a moment I could visualize myself in an Israeli jail! I tried to explain I had simply forgotten about the bag, which was packed in my suitcase, and after a few minutes (It seemed like hours) she told me I could return to my place in the line.

I hurried to the plane for the trip home.

Later, back home, I showed the little oil lamp replica to my Sunday School class, but I did not tell them the story of my lying to the Israeli security agent.

CHAPTER 20
ICELAND

The busy times of the 2014 holidays had subsided. *Now what?* I wondered. I still enjoyed traveling, even at age eighty-two, but my friends were not interested in joining me.

On a dreary winter day, I finished eating my lunch, then opened the newspaper and looked through my mail. A small brochure from Overseas Adventure Travel ("OAT") caught my attention. "UNTAMED ICELAND" seemed to leap off the page.

Wow! I did my research and quickly booked a trip for July 18th, 2015. I flew toReykjavik, Iceland, and joined 14 others in a meeting hall close to the airport. After our guide, a young woman who was half French and half Icelandic, introduced us to Icelandic culture, we first explored the area that the author, Jules Verne, had mentioned as the entry point for his *Journey to the Center of the Earth*.

We then traveled to a yellow sand beach and drove along a rocky coastline. While at lunch in an abandoned fishing village, the guide advised us, with a twinkle in her eye, to keep an eye out for the tiny elves and *huldufolk* (hidden people) that are said to live in this area. After lunch, we visited a shark farmer and tasted a national delicacy, *hakarl*, made from aged shark meat, followed by a chaser of potato liquor.

We also sailed in beautiful Breidafjordur Bay, viewed the myriad birds, and ate fresh seafood that was dredged up as we sailed. Yes, raw scallops are very tasty. Next was the Eiriksstadir Museum and the story of Vikings Leif Eiriksson and his son Eric the Red, who are credited as being the first settlers of Iceland. They arrived with the Irish women they had captured during their marauding.

One of my favorite stops was a local horse farm. Icelandic horses are a unique breed, small in size and a cheery disposition. They are patient, brave, smart, and possess a very smooth gait. A rider proved this by mounting one of the horses and then, holding a full glass of foaming beer, rode by the onlookers, while spilling nary a drop.

We visited Godafoss (Icelandic for Waterfall of the Gods) where I decided to join a few brave people in climbing up a rocky path to a cave situated behind the falling water. Halfway up, when the stone steps dissolved into a rocky path, I realized it may not have been a good idea for an 82-year-old, but too late, I was committed. Once there, after I caught my breath, I experienced an amazing sight through the waterfall, viewing the pool below, the shores of the river, and the parking lot.

After breakfast the next day, we visited the picturesque village of Dalvik. Donning foul-weather gear, we sailed out into the harbor to look for minke and humpback whales, dolphins, and porpoises. We saw a couple of whales, but no dolphins.

Returning to Reykjavik, we circumnavigated what in Iceland is called "The Golden Circle." The land there is in an area of hot springs. It is so warm that many locals bake their bread by burying it in the ground. Highways in this area never need to be plowed, because the warm ground keeps the roads clear of snow and ice.

Beneath Iceland there is a major geologic rift between two tectonic plates, European and North American. Heat from the Earth's center rises through the rift and warms the land. As the rift continues slowly to widen; one wonders what the future may hold for that area.

Courtesy of a handsome pilot, four of us took a side trip to Greenland, a massive area surrounded by icebergs.

Sue, pilot, and helicopter taken from Iceland to Greenland

Icebergs off the coast of Greenland

The next day we drove to the coast and viewed the black sand beaches. We bounced through an off-road super jeep ride, up the side of a cliff where the huge rock formations were like a scene from a science-fiction film. During World War II this elevated area was used for "early warning detection" radar that could indicate an enemy approaching by air.

It wouldn't be a trip to Iceland without a soak in the man-made Blue Lagoon, a hot spring with healing waters. Our guide had arranged an afternoon musical concert at her church, followed by dinner in the home of a local family.

We learned about their jobs, the children's school, and local politics. Their life didn't seem too different from mine. At the farewell dinner at our hotel, the Hilton Nordica, our group exchanged pictures and home addresses. Our driver for the trip was a delivery milkman, who had already made his early morning round.

He drove us around the Reykjavik area. He was very friendly and suggested I buy a horsehair bracelet and special soap at the horse farm. After downing a few Brennivin (black death, a popular alcoholic drink), he put his arm around my shoulder. *Wow! Was he coming on to me?*

When I gave his hand a little squeeze, he said, "You remind me so much of my mother."

CHAPTER 21
SECOND MARRIAGE AT 85

One Sunday after church, I was sitting in my recliner reading a book when I began to reflect on my life. I had been a single woman for over forty years and liked my life. My seven grandchildren brought me much joy. I had tried online dating, but it wasn't for me. Besides enjoying traveling, I played bridge once a week and had weekly classes at The Huntington YMCA. Yoga and water exercise were my favorites, as well as the sauna.

"Colors to remember," my yoga instructor would say, "are red, orange yellow, green, blue, purple, and white. Each color represents a type of vibration."

Yoga on the beach was my best-loved time. Warm sand under my towel and the sound of the waves lapping at the shore calmed my busy mind. Looking up through tree branches, I would watch fluffy white cumulus clouds drifting across the blue sky. Even the birds voiced their appreciation. Hearing the gulls at the beach caused me to feel and see the color lavender, which combined the stability of blue and the energy of red. Each yoga session ended with our bowing to one another and saying "Namaste." In Sanskrit it means "I bow to you." It evokes a feeling of oneness in heart and spirit.

After seeking advice and consultation about a new car, I bought a 2015 KIA Sorento. Though my days of needing a large-sized car were past, I did enjoy the many advantages of a station wagon/Suburban automobile.

Still wanting something else to think about, I decided to repaint the kitchen/family room. My son told me the name of a woman he consulted with at Sherwin Williams paint store. As a favor to him, she came to my house, studied the area and agreed to keep the stipple effect on the off-white ceiling and then said, "I can visualize painting the soffits black" (a soffit is a space between the top of the kitchen cabinets and the ceiling). At first, I didn't go for that but I trusted her expertise.

The room was large, 15 by 32 feet and was a combination kitchen/family room. It had a big picture window, two double-hung windows, an entrance door from outside, double sliding doors to the living-room/dining room, and a large, well-used fireplace, so there wasn't much wall area. "How about painting that space a burnt orange color?"

She did remark it would be a bold step.

When the painters arrived, I went shopping. Upon my return, painter's drop cloths covered all entrances. The painter pulled aside one of the cloths and said, "You are going to love it or hate it."

I loved it! It did not bring Halloween to mind at all. There was already oak hardwood flooring that started at the front of the house, and ran though the living room, dining room and kitchen/family room. Done!

So, a new car, redecorating, the house was in order, I had a fine family ... now what? I was in my eighties and was wondering about the next chapter of my life. Suddenly, **THE PHONE RANG.**

A deep, male voice said, "Susanah, this is George Pratt from the Community Church."

I knew he sang in the choir, but he added, "I am the President of the congregation," and he explained the Church had received an invitation to attend a fund-raising event for Erase Racism at the Garden City Hotel. Two tickets fully paid.

The President of Erase Racism was Elaine Gross. I had several opportunities to work with Elaine, a member of our church. She had devoted herself to organizing and implementing the work of Erase Racism.

George felt the church should be represented at the event, and he had asked the church secretary to accompany him, but she was not available. She had suggested my name, and George called to ask if I was willing to accompany him.

I happily accepted the invitation and had to admit I was impressed when a really nice car pulled into the driveway with a special license plate, (1-USJ). He was taller and more handsome than I remembered. We enjoyed the evening.

The next week, the church planned to show a movie. I answered "yes" when George asked me if I planned on attending the movie, and then he asked if I would like to have dinner with him before the movie. Again, I said "yes."

With such a full life, I was not eager to take on a new relationship. Nevertheless, I did enjoy being with George and we had several dates together. We enjoyed many of the same activities: concerts, plays, family gatherings, dinners, and local attractions.

When George asked me to marry him in late December of 2016, I said "no." His wife had died just seven months earlier. I knew he needed time to grieve.

He replied, "I am a man who knows his own mind and I have patience. But I will not ask you again."

I thought about it some more and told him that I would have an answer by his birthday in May. We continued to see each other and discovered we had much in common. Our church was a common bond, but also our love for our families. He had four children, as did I. All were self- sufficient and did not live at home. Our houses seemed too large for one person, and we were 84 and 89 years old.

I was in Hicks Nursery in Westbury and saw a garden flag that said, *Bless Our Nest*, so that was his birthday present, and my answer was "YES!"

She said "Yes"

"How about this summer, July?" was his next question.

There was much to do but we had planned a small, family ceremony and the pastor was our friend. My granddaughter Jessica was getting married in December and her nephew, Nicholas, was going to be her ring bearer.

Nicholas asked me if he could be our ring bearer, also.

I explained it was going to be a small wedding.

George intervened by saying, "Let's have Nicholas hold our rings and at the appropriate time, he can bring them up to the altar."

We wrote our own vows for the ceremony. George recounted our courtship, including my answer of "No" to his proposal. When the pastor asked if anyone wanted to share a story, George's son spoke up, saying he felt he was partially responsible for this marriage.

As a joke, for a Christmas present, he had given his dad a copy of *Dating for Dummies Over 60*.

George's niece, Kelly, spoke and wished us much happiness. She added, "Sue, you had me after you told George NO to his marriage proposal."

As a lawyer and judge, he wasn't often refused a request.

Wedding, Sue and George Pratt, July 20, 2017

There were many decisions to make, first a prenuptial agreement. Then, where would we live? Should we sell both houses and buy a condo? Maybe we should move to Florida? But we really didn't want to leave Long Island. Should we decide to live in one of our present homes?

My two-story house, one-car garage, and largest bedroom on the second floor (stairs to climb) didn't work too well with our advancing years. George's house had a two-car garage, a lovely setting, and we could live on one floor, with some modifications. It was close to our doctors, church, a good hospital, and family.

We chose George's house. With the help of his daughters, much of the furniture and decorations were taken away. Slowly, we have made it our home. The main problem was ownership. We should have sold both houses and then bought this house together. Nevertheless, so far, it has been six years of wonderful married life.

As I came to these forks on the road, I didn't know if I was making good decisions. But we all face these conditions and have to rely on our experience. Faith or whatever has guided us in the past will guide us in the future.

CHAPTER 22

OUR ONE-YEAR WEDDING ANNIVERSARY!

George and I decided to celebrate our one-year anniversary by taking a sailing trip on the four-masted Windstar, guest capacity 148. The ship left from Costa Rica, sailed south along the Pacific coastline with ports of call along the way, and thence to the Panama Canal.George discovered he enjoyed traveling just for pleasure.

We visited San Jose's incredible National parks, enjoyed learning about how coffee is grown, processed, and sold. I enjoyed tasting the many flavors at a coffee bar. Our guide introduced us to Costa Rica's history, including their struggle to remain a free, independent country.

Our stateroom was even nicer than we had expected. The food and the delightful salt air relaxed us. George was born and grew up on Keuka Lake, located in the finger lakes region of Upstate New York. Sailing was one of his favorite things to do.

Ironically, during our three days aboard the Windstar, there was not enough wind for them even to unfurl the sails. We soon learned there are major differences between fresh and salt water sailing. George had never seen a Zodiac, a safe, rigid, inflatable and seaworthy boat that has many uses. We used one to go ashore from the large 148-foot Windstar.

George is over six feet tall. I worried (smiled) as he carefully went down the swaying ramp and climbed aboard the bobbing Zodiac. Although the water was fairly calm, the small waves caused constant motion for the Zodiac.

The water was warm and inviting for a swim. We took a stroll along the beach and saw small, stone sculptures, made from local stones. A small boat provided transportation into the quiet harbor. We waved at a Coast Guard boat patrolling the area. Porpoises kept us company as we viewed the shoreline and hills and trees beyond.

A delicious "tropical Isle" lunch was waiting, set beneath the palm trees on the beach. After lunch, lounge chairs called out to us to take a nap. We took a stroll on the beach, seeing more small stone sculptures, and took a quick dip in the water before we returned to the Windstar.

Our journey took us south, along the Central America region but still part of North America, towards the Panama Canal. Along the way we stopped and visited a National Park, and saw incredible birds and animals up close. In a large garden area, hanging from small trees, were more than a hundred humming-bird feeders. It seemed that they were all in use, the tiny wings moving so rapidly you could not see them move.

We visited an animal hospital for injured and sick wild creatures. The caretaker held an orphaned sloth. The arms of the sloth were wrapped around the keeper's neck. It was a beautiful place, with more than 1400 types of wild orchids.

We continued sailing towards the Panama Canal, arriving in the early evening. The Windstar took its place in line for our appointed time. The fee for using the canal is determined by the length of the boat. The fee for the Windstar was $83,000.

The canal is now over 100 years old. Its construction cost the lives of 25,000 people, mostly from Malaria. As it connects two oceans you would think it would be salt water. In fact, it is not, but is fresh water, supplied by seventeen artificial interconnected freshwater lakes.

All different-size boats use the canal, from small rowboats to the large container ships. The Windstar created an unusual profile, and many observers watched us from the Miraflores Visitors Center.

We ended our trip in Panama City, in a beautiful and very modern hotel with amazing views, including the line of ships waiting their turn to enter the canal. The line stretched out until it disappeared over the horizon.

CHAPTER 23
ALASKA

ALASKA, our 50th and largest state, is located in the Northwestern part of North America. I have been favored with three separate trips there, each of them different from the others.

ALASKA TRIP # 1

THE PHONE RANG. It was my Aunt Estella, calling from Battle Creek, Michigan in 2005. "How would you like to go to Alaska with me to celebrate my ninetieth birthday?"

I said I would love to do that, and I suggested we take Tauck Tours.

Estella and my cousin Jeanne met me at the ship. On our first night, we made our way to the dining room, stopping by the small bar for a cocktail. My Aunt asked the young barkeeper if he had "Black velvet whiskey."

He nodded and poured her a drink.

I lifted my glass to Aunt Stella and said, "Happy ninetieth birthday".

She glared at me and said, "It isn't necessary to mention my age."

But each evening, the bartender dutifully poured her a Black Velvet whiskey. Our ship was considered small by cruise ship standards, but it was perfect for sailing closer to the shore. An on-board naturalist showed us how to look for "golf balls" in the trees, that were the white heads of Eagles resting there.

The captain, a very tall and personable man, was always accessible to chat or answer our questions. As we sailed into a fjord (a long, deep body of water carved by glaciers), he brought the ship close to the shore, putting the bow under a melting glacier waterfall so that we could collect the fresh water for us to drink.

As our boat turned around to return to the inland water passage, there was a HUGE cruise ship just entering the fjord. The Captain smiled and said "Well, there goes the neighborhood." Our first stop was the city of Haines. I had read about a craft store there that had native jewelry. My relatives declined to accompany me, so I decided to go alone. After a quick look at the Haines library, I found the jewelry shop and quickly picked out a ring and a bracelet. They were silver, with black background.

The design was the heads of an eagle and a falcon. Folklore said they represent the eye of the eagle and the wisdom of the falcon. As the captain announced the departure, my frantic Aunt explained Sue was not on board.

He replied, "Sorry, but this dock space is dedicated to the next ship." He patted her hand and said," We will go out into the harbor, and I will send a tender (small boat) back to the dock area to pick her up."

Running my best and breathing hard, I managed to just make the gangplank before it was removed.

ALASKA TRIP #2

THE PHONE RANG. Cheryl and Linda wanted to know if I would be interested in going to Alaska with them and their husbands, Chris and Sam.

Granddaughter Sarah wanted to go, too, and she needed a roommate. Sarah and I had shared many adventures together so I knew this would be fun. It would be on a large cruise ship with many interesting things to do and see.

The decor of the ship was dazzling, the food was exceptional, and the company delightful. Each evening there was entertainment. My favorite was hearing a trainer/driver talk about the *Iditarod* (means distant) dog sled race. She brought two puppies, one a Siberian husky and the other an Alaskan malamute. They are the only breeds allowed to participate in the race.

She discussed her book, autographed Sarah's copy, and let us hold, ever so briefly, one of the puppies.

ALASKA TRIP #3

Can you believe my third journey to Alaska, in 2017, was as a new bride, at age eighty-four? George's twin daughters have a business that breeds and trains Golden Retrievers. They were planning on attending a seminar onboard a cruise ship to Alaska and invited us to join them.

Most memorable was our airplane view of the south face of Denali Mountain, once known as Mount McKinley. A 6-seater plane flew us near the top of the mountain. The pilot flew past it in both directions, so each passenger side of the plane had its own view.

Denali (formerly Mount McKinley) viewed from the air

The day was chilly, clear, and sunny. We could see for miles—the wild Alaska mountains, valleys, and rivers, and no sign of humanity whatsoever. Suddenly, an unexpected turbulence caused the plane to drop. George's head hit the ceiling.

Everyone was okay, but I silently wondered *"What if the pilot's head hit the ceiling frame and it knocked him unconscious?"* We would have been helpless and would probably crash, lost forever on Denali's frozen slopes. Fortunately, that did not happen, and after we landed safely, we visited the home of the Iditarod dogs.

We even had an exciting ride in a wheeled cart pulled by a team of six dogs. Near the end of the ride, George and I looked at each other and wondered *What will be next in our new journey through life?*

CHAPTER 24
REFLECTIONS

Life is a journey, not a destination, a metaphor often credited to Ralph Waldo Emerson. Now that I am "pushing 90 years of age," I would add "and you have many choices to make on how you will travel your journey."

My life, like many others, has been abundant with many opportunities. As my old memories have been stirred while writing this book, I am amazed at my ability to remember details. Over the years, my lifestyle has changed drastically from a young girl, to a bride, a mother of four, to the only person in charge of our family.

Dr. Spock, although an American pediatrician, also studied Psychoanalysis. In 1943, he wrote a book about Baby and Child Care. I remember it was almost my bible for understanding and living with children.

Besides my mom, my other sources on how to raise children were limited to newspaper and magazine articles. Humorist Erma Bombeck wrote a delightful column about suburban home life. Amy Vanderbilt, although considered an expert on etiquette, often wrote about gracious living. She introduced me and many others to another way of living.

Reader's Digest magazine had monthly features, like "Life in These United States" and "Laughter, the Best Medicine". I shared many stories of my experiences with my "koffee klatch" neighbors (a social gathering for conversation). Two of my favorite stories were about a roasting pan and black crayons.

1. A young bride was preparing a boneless ham for dinner. Her new husband watched with interest. "Why did you cut off the tip of the ham before you put it in the pan?" She replied, "I don't know. My mother always did." She asked her mother and learned it was because her mother had always done it. They next asked Grandma, who explained, "My roasting pan was too short for the ham."
2. When a mother was asked at her first pre-school conference why her son only drew pictures in black crayons, she had no answer. "Let's ask him." His answer was simple. I sit in the back of the room and by the time it is my turn to go up to the crayon box in the front of the room, only black crayons are available."

It amazes me to hear these same stories being repeated even now, three generations later.

Do you remember the saying, Too Soon Old, Too Late Smart"?

At age forty, I took the fork in the road that led to being a strong, independent woman, and then remarried at age 85. Now fifty years later, in retrospect, I marvel at the journey I have enjoyed. My children have made good decisions. They are all still married with wonderful families. It does truly "take a village to raise a child." They have been influenced by family, members of our community, the schools, educational opportunities, and a law system that tries to help in times of serious trouble.

Oddly, telephone calls have introduced me to most of the major changes in my life—a plane accident, a lawyer named Lee Kreindler, the library, where I found a career, and George.

Change is a major feature of living. It is always with us. Success comes from our ability to adjust to and anticipate change. Most of all, love is a major part of life, with faith and belief in seeking help while on your own life journey.

God has been in my long life, and it is my faith that has helped me. Take some time to ponder the vicissitudes of life. When you focus on problems, you'll have more problems. When you focus on possibilities, you'll have more opportunities.

How do I make decisions? One way is to gather as many facts as possible, review those facts, and then make the decision. Later, if you learn you need to make a change, do it! At the time you made the original decision, you thought it was the right one. If it turns out wrong, or if the circumstances change, then re-evaluate and move on!

When I was in Israel, the guide suggested that, when we left our hotel we should take with us their business card with the hotel's name, address, and phone number printed on it. If we got lost, we could just use a taxi to return to our hotel. (Good advice for any place and any time.)

Like Theodore Geisel, aka Dr. Seuss, once said, "DON'T CRY BECAUSE IT IS OVER; SMILE BECAUSE IT HAPPENED.

In reflecting on my long life, it occurred to me that airplanes and boats have been important features of the many varied experiences I have enjoyed.

I remember my grandfather saying as a young man he "drove" a fancy two-wheeled cart (horse and buggy) and thought he was quite a dandy. And he lived long enough to fly to New York in a propeller-driven plane to see his great-grandchildren. Two generations after that I was privileged to enjoy the many other advances in air travel by jet planes.

I had my first airplane ride when I was in seventh grade at the University of Florida's P.K. Yonge Laboratory school. An upper classmate was interested in my brother. She "became" my friend and hung out with me, i.e. to see my brother. She had a pilot's license and invited me to go flying with her in a Piper Cub. My Mother wrote to my dad for advice. The day for the flight came and there had been no answer from Dad. I begged her to allow me to go, and she did.

We took off from a small airport and flew low over Gainesville, Florida. As we buzzed my house, (that means to turn off the engine and then restart it, which can cause a loud bang), I could see Mom in the yard waving a dish towel. What I couldn't see was the letter she clutched in her left hand from Dad, saying, "No, I don't think she should do this."

This event gave birth to a life-long delight in flying, particularly in small planes. Of course, I have flown in many commercial jets, but among my flights in small planes were:

My son-in-law's best friend Leffie took me for rides in an old Tecumseh, (a small two-seater plane) he had assembled from a box of parts. We flew south from Tampa, over small lakes and rural country dotted with palm trees and orchards of orange trees. When you are looking down from a plane, the view is very different from what you see on the ground.

A sight-seeing trip around Alaska's Mount McKinley's south face. No sign of civilization anywhere.

A twin-engine plane ride to the Caribbean Island of Virgin Gorda. We landed on what looked like a small, paved road.

An aerial view of the Finger Lakes region in upstate New York. It was in a four-seater pontoon plane.

A float plane (with pontoons) that landed on a lake in Alaska.

If I wanted to choose one most memorable flight experience, without a doubt, it would be the hot-air balloon ride I had in Kenya, which I have described elsewhere in this book as part of my trip to Africa.

In addition to the small-plane rides, I have delighted in several helicopter trips:

From Long Island to Manhattan, landing on a postage-stamp size spot near the United Nations.

On a clear and beautiful day, a young female Hualapai Indian expertly flew us in a helicopter down into the Grand Canyon. We climbed aboard a Zodiac (a small inflatable boat) with a young, male Hualapai Indian, who guided us down the Colorado River. The geologist on board explained how a small stream began to cut a channel through the layers of rock. Five to six million years later, the stream, now a river, had carved out and continues to deepen the Canyon. We saw the flora and fauna of the area. "Look up," the geologist suggested, "and see the bat caves. Their droppings, guano, are an excellent source of fertilizer, but it is almost inaccessible for harvesting." We came ashore just short of Lake Powell.

The helicopter pilot who flew four of us from Reykjavik, Iceland, over the Denmark Straight to Greenland was competent and daring. Greenland has very large icebergs, and he flew low enough so we could easily see the blueish-green colors in the icebergs that floated in the brilliant blue water. Later, we would kayak close enough to an iceberg to almost touch it. Of course, most of the iceberg was below the surface of the water.

I have had commercial air flights in Alaska and Italy, China and Scandinavia, Spain and Morocco, Argentina and South America, and Florida and British Columbia.

An Air China jet plane flew me non-stop from New York's J.F.K. International airport to China's Shanghai Pudong international airport.

Will my next flight be with Elon Musk to outer space?

In my many travels, I have been privileged to ride on many boats varying widely in size, type and age. Among them: a cruise ship on the Yangtze River in China; a Sampan in China; a Felucca, (a small Egyptian boat) across the Nile River; a Hovercraft from England to France; and a "trip to nowhere" aboard the Queen Elizabeth 2.

I have fished on a boat with Charlie in Michigan, taken a lake tour of Keuka Lake, sailed on a three-masted schooner through the Panama Canal, and been on River cruises of the Upper and Lower Mississippi. And I still remember my Sunfish ride on Keuka Lake, my times on Jean Butler's boat for cocktails in Oyster Bay Harbor, and a bare-boat charter on a schooner in the Virgin Islands.

There was the Circle Line trip around Manhattan with Forrest and Moira Parkinson, the dinner cruise around New York's lower harbor celebrating George's 90th birthday and our first wedding anniversary. And let's not forget the Staten Island Ferry to the Statue of Liberty.

Most unforgettable was the Stephen Tauber cruise out of Rockland, Maine to mark my 65th birthday, Over the years, there were also various Zodiac trips (ship to shore and back), as well as a tender from the American Constitution to shore at Newport, another cruise ship on the Hudson River from New York City to Albany and back and a cruise ship ride around Cape Cod.

New York Harbor is one of the largest natural harbors in the world, located at the mouth of the Hudson River. In 1885, as a gesture of international friendship, France gave to the United States of America, a 40-foot-tall sculpture they called "La Liberty declarant is monde" (Liberty enlightening the world). It was shipped in pieces and, due to lack of funds, stored on Bedloe Island, in upper New York harbor.

Two years later, the gift was assembled and installed, also on Bedloe Island, which in 1956, was renamed Liberty Island. A secret box under the statue contains a copy of the U.S. Constitution, a portrait of designer Frederic Bartholdi, artist, and twenty bronze medals.

I have sailed by this amazing object on various types of ships: an ocean liner (the QE2), the Staten Island ferry, a sailboat, and a dinner yacht. I have flown over it and even climbed up to the crown. One year, I welcomed in the New Year at this most impressive sight.

In 2018, I was viewing this marvelous statue again. This time I stood holding hands with my husband of one year. To celebrate a combination of George's 90th birthday and our first wedding anniversary, we chartered a ship for a dinner cruise.

With about fifty guests, including many from our two families, as well as a number of our best friends, we boarded the ship at Pier 61 on the Hudson River in the late afternoon. The ship carried us north to view the Intrepid Museum, and then turned south on the river, past the New York City skyline and around the office towers on Lower Manhattan. We then turned up the East River, passing under, in order, the Brooklyn, Manhattan, and Williamsburg Bridges, BMW" for short.

We then turned back down the river and moved off to Liberty Island to get a close-up view of the Statue. During this inspiring cruise around New York Harbor, we were treated to a fine dinner, first to drinks and appetizers, followed by roast beef with all the trimmings.

As a special treat and in celebration of our first wedding anniversary, the Captain invited George and me to the "bridge" toward the bow of the ship, from which we looked up-close at Lady Liberty, straight ahead of us. Our friends and family really appreciated this special celebration.

George and I also enjoyed a short autumn cruise to view the foliage on the upper Mississippi River. Who knew we would, soon after, cruise the lower Mississippi, from Memphis to New Orleans?

On July 4th, 2020, during the New Orleans end of our second Mississippi River cruise, we watched fireworks over the river, while sitting on our small, private deck of the cruise ship. We talked about the struggles during the Civil War battle at Vicksburg and the American Revolution and we mused that our freedom is not free, but it has been earned by the sacrificial efforts of many.

Our next river cruise, in 2021, was along the Hudson River to Albany, New York, and it included all the sights along the way. Departing from the busy harbor of New York, we sailed under the George Washington Bridge and were soon enjoying the beautiful scenery of the magnificent Hudson Valley.

In 2022, we took another cruise, leaving from Boston Harbor. We stopped at Gloucester, Plymouth, Martha's Vineyard, Newport, New Bedford and Provincetown. A riverboat is an easy and restful way to travel. Accommodations are sumptuous, the food is great, and there is no moving your luggage from one sleeping place to another.

CHAPTER 25
AND IN CONCLUSION

Originally, when I started writing this book, I thought this story would end with my marriage to George. But new events have suggested a little bit more. George had traveled extensively, but his trips were mostly work-related.

In the first few years of our marriage, George and I enjoyed traveling together. We visited some of his favorite places in upstate New York. Among my favorites were the ride on the Erie Canal, the feminist national park in Seneca Falls, ("The "park" consisted of a single building), a seaplane flight from Keuka Lake over the other Finger lakes, and meeting some of George's upstate friends. We were also honored at a special, lovely wedding reception with many family members coming all the way from Salt Lake City.

I did accompany George to an ABC television interview in New York City for filming of a documentary concerning one of his cases, the ABSCAM trials of corrupt congressmen. I also enjoyed accompanying him to an Arbitration Conference in Minneapolis, Minnesota. General Mills has a wonderful Visitors Center there, and spouses of the arbitrators were treated to a visit.

We learned that in 1921 Wheaties, and all other cereal flakes, had been accidentally discovered when a bit of bran gruel was dropped on a hot stove and produced a crispy flake. It became known as Wheaties, the Breakfast of Champions.

In the spring of 2017, we flew to Salt Lake City to attend the wedding of George's grandson, Eli, to Liz. During the trip, I was also introduced to Eli's two brothers and two sisters and their families. We all met again at a family vacation resort in New Hampshire on Squam Lake, (the filming location of the movie *On Golden Pond*) and I enjoyed getting to know the family a little better.

At breakfast the first day, Great-Grandson Samson, age about three, warily looked at me, then with the sweetest smile ever, he asked, "Can I sit in your lap?"

"Love you forever!"

Between us, George and I have a family of sixty. We each had four children, then their seven spouses, twelve grandchildren (all but two with spouses), and twenty great-grandchildren. Most of George's family live in Utah, with twin daughter Lise and Marcy & Jim Burke, who live in Virginia. Son "Duffy" and his wife Yanci live in Texas.

My family are on Long Island, except a daughter, Linda, and her husband Sam; my grandson, Lawrence, his wife Courtney and their daughter, Savannah, who live in Florida. My grandson Tyler, his wife Taylor and their son Samuel live in Texas.

Despite dealing with limited travel and some isolation due to Covid and other new diseases, George and I look forward to more life experiences. We agree that life is basically good, and we try to appreciate it every moment. Health issues, loving care, and increased awareness are indeed lessons to be learned.

When George realized his eyesight was failing, he voluntarily gave up driving and handed me the keys to his car. A few days later he presented me with a chauffeur's cap. The greatest and fundamental lesson is in developing an appreciation of your own life through faith and love.

EPILOGUE

Thanks for coming with me as I have tried to recall, however dimly, some of the events over the 90 years of my own life's journey. In August 2023 I celebrated my 90th birthday. What lies ahead for me? For George and me? For you? And for those you love?

As George and I sat on our deck and pondered these questions...
MY CELL PHONE RANG.

Susanah K. Pratt
One week after her 90th Birthday.
What's next?

www.ingramcontent.com/pod-product-compliance
Lightning Source LLC
Chambersburg PA
CBHW061736070526
44585CB00024B/2695